Read

Reading on Your Own

An Extensive Reading Course

Mary Ellen Barrett
The American University

Maryanne Kearny Datesman
Georgetown University

Heinle & Heinle Publishers
A Division of Wadsworth, Inc.
Boston, Massachusetts 02116 U.S.A.

Vice President and Publisher: Stanley J. Galek
Editorial Director: David C. Lee
Assistant Editor: Kenneth Mattsson
Project Manager: Stacey Sawyer, Sawyer & Williams
Production Supervisor: Patricia Jalbert
Manufacturing Coordinator: Lisa McLaughlin
Text Design: Nancy Benedict
Illustrations: Susan Detrich
Photo Research: Judy Mason
Cover Design: Jean Hammond
Cover Photo: © Andrew Brilliant/Carol Palmer, with thanks
      to the Trident Booksellers & Café, Boston

Manufactured in the United States of America.

Heinle & Heinle Publishers is a division of Wadsworth, Inc.

Library of Congress Cataloging-in-Publication Data

Barrett, Mary Ellen.
     Reading on your own : an extensive reading course /
Mary Ellen Barrett, Maryanne Kearny Datesman.
          p.   cm.
     ISBN 0-8384-2274-8
     1. English language—Textbooks for foreign speakers.
     2. Reading (Higher education) 3. College readers.   I.
Kearny Datesman, Maryanne.   II. Title.
     PE1128.B326   1992
     428.6'4—dc20   91-41485
                                                            CIP

ISBN 0-8384-2274-8

10 9 8 7 6 5 4 3 2 1

For George H. Datesman, Jr.
and
Marie C. Evans

Contents

Preface

Reading On Your Own is designed for high-intermediate to advanced learners of English as a second language. It is **not**, however, a traditional reading text. Rather, it is a design for a course in which students choose their own reading material—from newspapers, magazines, books, and even academic journals and textbooks—and read on their own. By using the approach presented in this text, students become empowered to read with more ease and confidence materials written for native speakers of English.

Course Design

Reading On Your Own is probably unlike any reading text you have used in the past. In many traditional ESL/EFL reading programs and texts, an entire unit is devoted to one or two readings, replete with comprehension and vocabulary exercises. In a real reading situation, however, students seldom do this kind of intensive analysis. Instead, they read with some purpose: as students, they must read textbooks or articles for academic classes; as professionals, they must read journals published in English to keep current; or simply as curious human beings, they enjoy reading and learning about the ideas and opinions of others.

We have, therefore, used activities that focus on global (extensive) reading strategies rather than on those that teach the more traditional reading subskills, although many of these are treated as a part of the act of reading. For instance, there are no "main idea" exercises, but students have to summarize each article they read and necessarily have to recognize the main idea. Likewise, there are no traditional "guessing vocabulary from context" exercises, but students are shown ways to read without constantly using a dictionary, and they do learn to use context clues.

Students use the reading selections in this text as a springboard for discussion and as practice for selecting and reading their own articles from a variety of sources. Part A in the text explains how the course is structured, how to do the course work, and how to use the library to find high-interest reading materials. From the beginning of the course, students select and read articles *they* want to read, and the text provides strategies for becoming better, more independent readers.

The remaining parts (B and C) provide further, more detailed practice in course and/or supplemental activities. Thus, the emphasis is on the *extensive* reading of materials the students select themselves, rather than on those articles found in the text. The course requires the students to read a lot and to use what they learn from their reading for writing, group discussions, and oral reports, all with the purpose of helping them to become independent readers.

In this way, the work of the course is both individualized and student-centered.

Students may choose readings from a variety of sources: newspapers, magazines, journals, or textbooks. Their main criterion for selecting a reading should be real interest in the subject. For example, one student may be interested in sports and choose to read articles from the local sports page or *Sports Illustrated*. A second may want to read exclusively about his or her country as it is represented in the American press. A third may be a graduate student whose interest is in articles on modern economic theory. Or, as is more typical, a student may choose to read about many subjects from many different sources. Students are also required to read one or two books—any kind, as long as they are books the students truly want to read. We have had some students, for instance, who became Agatha Christie fans and others who decided to read a novel in English that they had previously read in translation, and still others who avidly read critiques of computer programs! In this course, then, students do a *lot* of reading, and by doing so, improve not only their ability to read but also their confidence.

Course Rationale

The impetus for this course design was a lively plenary session at the 1984 Teachers of English to Speakers of Other Languages (TESOL) in New York, featuring Stephen Krashen, who spoke about the importance of reading to the achievement of academic success. He reported on studies done with American students that show that those young people who read for pleasure consistently did better on all measures of academic success than those who did not read for pleasure. Further, he mentioned research that demonstrates that good writers do more reading for their own pleasure and interest than do poor writers.

How, we pondered, could we tap into this concept in second-language learning, yet at the same time provide the structure that is necessary for an actual reading program? How could we incorporate Krashen's principles of second-language acquisition in such a course design? We have attempted to do this in the following ways:

1. Students are free to read anything that interests them, and they read a lot.

2. What they select to read is often slightly above their current level of competence. Because they are interested in the subject, they read it anyway.

3. Since the focus is on global language rather than on traditional reading skills, much of what is acquired is subconscious.

4. Students are interested in the subjects they choose to read about, so speaking and writing about them flow naturally from this interest.

5. Students are not penalized when they make errors in writing or speaking; rather, they are encouraged to express themselves freely. Thus, the affective filter is lowered.

Treatment of Vocabulary

The text also takes an unusual approach to vocabulary, the area that seems to present one of the greatest obstacles to fluency in reading. We have taken a three-tiered approach in vocabulary work.

1. For the text readings, we have provided simple glosses for the specialized words relating to the topic. The article serves as a vehicle for practice, and we want the student to understand it quickly. These glossed words may or may not become part of the students' passive vocabulary.

2. We have selected certain key words and expressions in each reading that appear over and over again in both popular and academic prose but that are probably unfamiliar to our students. We selected these vocabulary items as key terms because they are useful and because they can be defined from their context. In these practices, the students are given the context (1 or 2 sentences), and then asked to paraphrase the portion of the sentence containing the key word or expression. In this way, students gain experience in making use of contextual clues as well as in paraphrasing. Thus, these key words and expressions become part of the students' passive-recognition vocabulary.

3. For each Reading Report they do, students are required to choose words that they want to learn. They must look up their meanings and use them in an original sentence, thereby making these words part of their active vocabulary. In the Check Your Progress section of the lessons, we provide lists of words from the readings we feel would be valuable additions to the students' personal vocabulary lists. Students may choose from these words or select others that appeal to them from articles they have chosen on their own.

Acknowledgments

We are indebted to several people whose thinking influenced ours in the preparation of this manuscript. In particular, we would like to thank Martha Low of the University of Oregon, whose criticism was invaluable; Anne V. Martin of Syracuse University, whose work on "Bridging Vocabulary" affected our selection of vocabulary items; Judith Cook and Myra Shulman, our colleagues at The American University, whose work with our materials added several dimensions to the course, and Earl Stevick and Stephen Krashen, whose work is an inspiration. We would also like to express our appreciation to our families, whose patience and cooperation were endless. A special thanks goes to David Lee of Heinle & Heinle, who is an innovator.

M. E. B.
M. K. D.

To the Teacher: Organizing Activities in the Student-Centered Reading Course

Reading on Your Own: An Extensive Reading Course at a Glance

Level:

High Intermediate to Advanced

Type of Class:

Reading
Reading and Writing
Integrated Skills

Features:

- Integrates reading, writing, listening, and speaking skills
- Teaches students to read long articles and books without being dependent on their dictionaries
- Teaches students how to use the library to find books and magazine and journal articles
- Uses student-centered approach: structured small-group discussions, students choose their own reading materials

Activities Students Do:

- Locate and read three articles per week from newspapers, magazines
- Write a reading report on each article read
- Create their own individual vocabulary list of at least ten words per week, with definitions and original sentences
- Give an oral report to the class on one article every week or every other week
- Participate in small-group discussions of topics chosen and researched by the group members, and prepare group discussion report form each week
- Read at least one book, and prepare a book report on it during the course
- Read and discuss articles in this text, and practice extensive reading skills
- Practice summarizing and paraphrasing

Optional Activities:

- Evaluate readings for fact versus opinion
- Conduct debates
- Write a synthesis paper

Organization of the Text

The book is organized into three parts. Part A introduces the extensive reading course and its requirements and gives initial instruction in how to meet them. Its purpose is to provide an overview and get students started in the independent reading program. For this reason, Lessons 1, 2, and 3 should be completed during the first part of class. Lesson 4 can be deferred until shortly before the first book report is due.

The first order of business is for students to be able to write Reading Reports (readings can easily be found in newspapers or provided by the teacher, if necessary). Next, students find articles on what they really want to read. At this level, students are capable of talking about what they have read without initial formal instruction in group discussions. We have found that most students have had experience giving oral reports, but they do improve in organization and execution after doing Lesson B 3.

Part B contains more detailed instruction and practice in each of the course activities: acquiring vocabulary, writing Reading Reports, discussing readings, and reporting orally. Once the independent reading phase is underway, you (perhaps with your students) can choose the sequence in which to take these chapters, depending on the class's needs.

Part C includes supplemental activities. It is possible to conduct the course for a whole term without doing these lessons, but if time permits, they add a further dimension and provide specific purpose to reading activities. These lessons can also be done as the need or desire to use them arises.

Each lesson is thematically organized around a general topic, and any of these topics can be used for any of the activities. For example, the topic of the lesson on group discussion skills is abortion, a subject which also lends itself well to debate. The oral reporting lesson centers on paranormal phenomena, a topic that could also stimulate lively and interesting group discussions. So, after completing a lesson for its intended purpose, the topic then becomes available for a variety of other activities.

These activities require students to demonstrate not only that they have done the outside reading, but also that they can make use of the information. Because the emphasis is on understanding content, we recommend that grades be given on the basis of how much has been accomplished rather than on language usage. Students should be encouraged *to discuss and write freely* about what they have read without fear of being penalized for making mistakes. Of course, the teacher will sometimes feel it necessary to make corrections, but this should be done in a way that neither inhibits nor intimidates. Some students, however, strongly request that the language in their written reports be corrected.

READING REPORTS For each outside reading, the student is asked to submit a Reading Report that contains a statement of the main idea of the reading, a summary, a response to the content, and new vocabulary. These reports demonstrate to the teacher that the student has completed the assignment. We usually require that students attach photocopies

of the articles, particularly at the beginning of the term. To familiar-
ize students with the requirements and procedures of the course, it
is important to begin during the first week with Part A, Lessons 1, 2,
and 3, which deal with how to do the Reading Reports and vocabulary lists and how to find articles and books in the library. Lesson 4
on how to do a book report may be completed at a later time.

After the program gets underway, it is expected that students
will submit three reading reports each week (either on a reading
from this text and two outside readings, or on three outside readings). One outside reading should be on topics related to those
chosen for group reports that week. This may be the theme of the
lesson, one of the suggested topics at the end of each lesson, or a
topic suggested by the students. For the other readings, we encourage students to choose articles on topics in which they are truly
interested. If students are taking academic courses, one of these two
reading reports may be part of a chapter or an article assigned in
that course.

Evaluating Reading Reports   It is usually easy to tell if the student
has understood what has been read by what is written in the report
(even without a photocopy of the article). If all the parts of the Reading
Report have been completed, the student should be given credit for the
assignment. You may wish to rate how effective the Reading Report is
by using a plus or minus system. From time to time, you may also wish
to assign a Reading Report on a particular article in this text or on one
you bring in and duplicate for the students as a ''test'' of
comprehension.

Explain to the students that these reports are evaluated on the
basis of content, not on writing skills or grammar. You may choose
to correct selected errors (or all of them, as the students frequently
request!), but the important part of the assignment should always be
whether the student has understood the material and what he or she
has to say about it in the response. At the beginning, some students
tend to copy directly from their articles. If you emphasize that the
summaries should be in their own words so that you will know that
they understood the article, you may be able to avoid this problem.
You will find that the reports improve dramatically with practice.

GROUP REPORTS   Students are asked to select what they want to discuss from a list of
topics, either from among those suggested in the text or from others
that arise from class discussion. Or, you may announce that there
will be group discussions and ask for suggestions for topics from the
students. As students brainstorm the topics, you list them on the
board. Groups of three to five students then form around the topics
chosen for that week (you may ask everyone interested in each topic
to stand and form a group). The groups may wish to meet briefly to
decide which kind of article each will find or to limit their topic.

On the day of the group discussion, each group meets to
exchange the information from their articles and to formulate a
report to be given orally at the next class meeting. Each student
should, in turn, present his or her article to the others in the group.
Because the students have read a variety of articles, the information
each student reports should emphasize the facts, opinions, or
approaches stated in his or her article. The group report should then

integrate information and reflect the discussion the students had about the common topic.

One student acts as the "recorder" who writes up the discussion, and another reports the findings to the class. Both, of course, are revolving duties. Group reports should be informal, with all members of the group assisting the reporter, and members of the class should be encouraged to ask questions or make comments. This is an activity which should be done regularly, at least once every two weeks, depending on how frequently your class meets.

Evaluating Group Reports   We recommend that group activities be evaluated on level of participation rather than on quality. If a student is present, prepared with an article, and takes part in the discussion, he or she should receive credit for having done the assignment. Those who *don't* do any one of these should not. The point of the activity is to encourage students to share and make use of what they have read.

INDIVIDUAL ORAL REPORTS

Another way to focus on information acquired from reading is to ask students to give a short (5 to 8 minutes) oral report on their outside reading. As with the group reports, this activity should be done on a regular basis. Perhaps one day a week could be set aside as oral report day with half the students reporting one week, and the other half the next. We have had success by encouraging students to report on the most interesting reading they have done in a two-week period. Even those students whose oral skills are weak can keep the interest of the rest of the class if their topic is intriguing enough.

Evaluating Oral Reports   Once again, the purpose of this activity is to focus on information acquired through reading. If the student shows evidence of preparation and presents the report, credit should be given for the assignment. If time permits, you may wish to comment on one problem (pronunciation, word choice, etc.) for each person.

GRADES AND EVALUATION

Most programs require that students receive some type of a grade. Using this text and the independent reading system does not preclude the administration of grades, even though individual work is not graded and tests are not given. We suggest a contract system—the student must complete a certain amount of work to pass the course, more to get a B, and more yet to get an A. It has to be made clear to students from the beginning what must be done to receive a particular grade.

As an example, following is an excerpt from the handout we give students to explain the course requirements, which can be modified to meet the needs of your students or program. For instance, you may wish to vary the number of vocabulary words required each week, or, for less advanced classes, you might want to require only one book report. The possible permutations of the sample requirements are endless. We do recommend, however, that to achieve the best results, you require three Reading Reports each week.

Sample Student Handout

Course Requirements

To pass this course with a grade of C, the following assignments must be successfully completed each week:

1. Three Reading Reports:
    a. one on an article for group discussion
    b. one on an article of particular interest to you
    c. one on an academic or serious article

Reading Reports must include the vocabulary section. At least 10 vocabulary words must be defined and used in sentences.

2. As assigned:
    a. textbook reading and exercises
    b. oral reports on readings
    c. participation in both group discussions and group reports

3. You must also read one fiction or nonfiction book during the first half of the term, and another during the second half.

To receive a grade of B, you must read one additional book and three additional articles, for which you submit Reading Reports.

To receive a grade of A, you must read two additional books and six additional articles.

Almost all of the readings will be selected by you. It is your responsibility to prepare a Reading Report Form for each article or book. In this course, both the articles you read and the vocabulary work are individualized. The Reading Reports will not be evaluated for grammar or spelling, but rather for completeness and content. If you are asked to redo a report, it will not be credited until both the first and second versions are returned. If you are not present for an assigned group discussion and report or for an oral report, you will not be credited for that assignment. There will be no tests. Your final grade will be based on how successful you are in demonstrating that you have read and understood the assignments.

For those teachers who may be concerned about not giving traditional reading assignments and tests and therefore not having the usual means of assessing student progress, we suggest administering a standardized measure—such as the Nelson Test—at the beginning and again at the end of the term. We think you will be, as we were, pleasantly surprised at the progress your students have made, not only in reading but also in general language skills.

Assuming a fourteen-week semester and a class that meets every day for an hour to an hour and a half, we have found the following weekly schedule to be workable.

Monday	Tuesday	Wednesday	Thursday	Friday
Text Work	Group Discussion and Preparation of Group Reports	Group Reports	Oral Reports	Text work and Planning

Once the students understand the system and the course is underway, the teacher has little planning to do. However, as you may have surmised, there is a great deal of paperwork and book-keeping as well as continuing in-class interaction and monitoring of discussion. While we have found that there is no "quick and dirty" way to expedite the evaluation of Reading Reports, we can suggest a method of keeping track of the students' work. We use the following grid to check in the work as it is completed and to record participation in group work.

Name _____

Reading Reports

Type of Reading

	Week 1	Week 2	Week 3	Week 4
Newspaper				
Journal				
Popular magazine				
Serious magazine				
Textbook				
Special assignment				

	Week 5	Week 6	Week 7	Week 8
Newspaper				
Journal				
Popular magazine				
Serious magazine				
Textbook				
Special assignment				

	Week 9	Week 10	Week 11	Week 12
Newspaper				
Journal				
Popular magazine				
Serious magazine				
Textbook				
Special assignment				

Books								
Extra articles								
Oral reports								
Group reports								

We prepare a file folder for each student with the grid stapled to the inside. As Reading Reports are evaluated, they are checked in and placed in the file for the entire term. Files are returned to students each week so that they can look at their reports and make sure they are up-to-date with their work. Adding each week's work to the file enables students to see how much work they have done (or not done). Students can also see the progress they are making in improving the quality of their reports. It also helps to resolve any discrepancies between what has been credited and what may be claimed. At the end of the term, the file is returned to the student.

We further suggest holding conferences with your students two to three times during the term to discuss matters such as the quality of their Reading Reports, their selection of readings, and their progress in general. We set aside an occasional "free reading" day, when students have a chance to go through their files or simply read while we talk with them individually.

Implementing the Text

PART A, LESSON 1

1. There is a lot of information here, and you may need to explain the course structure several times. Remember, the whole concept is new to students, and even with clear handouts on how the course is set up, it usually takes a couple of explanations.

2. It's a good idea to explain the pedagogical rationale for this approach to the students. Some students are entrenched in the idea that you need to have a book that tells you exactly what to do in order to learn, so it's hard for them to believe that they can become better readers just by reading. It is not necessary to explain Krashen's theory of language learning in detail. But, it is important for them to know that there is evidence that this system works and that they are responsible for their own success or failure in making it work.

PART A, LESSON 2

1. For the readings at the very beginning of the term (before Lesson A 3, which explains how to find articles in the library), encourage students to use newspapers or news magazines as sources for their articles. In English-speaking countries, these kinds of publications are readily available. Teachers in non-English-speaking countries can bring any books, magazines, and newspapers that are available from school or personal sources to class and allow the students to choose articles according to their interests.

2. In experimenting with this course, from time to time we have also asked students to subscribe to a news magazine or newspaper (at reduced classroom rates) for outside reading. We have found that this helps, particularly at the beginning, in being able to evaluate whether students have written accurate summaries. It also eliminates the need to attach photocopies to Reading Reports.

3. You will need to bring a stack of magazines to class to practice reading titles and captions to predict the content of articles.

4. Don't be discouraged if early attempts at paraphrasing consist largely of synonyms with few true changes in wording. Simply point this out to your students, and keep encouraging them to "put it in their own words." Assure them that they won't be

penalized for making mistakes. Eventually, you will see significant improvement.

5. The following grammar tips for paraphrasing may be helpful to your students: 1. active/passive voice change (We must reset our body clocks. → Our body clocks must be reset.) 2. word form change (New research suggests that . . . → Suggestions made by researchers . . .), 3. phrase/clause structure change (a hot bath → bathing in hot water) 4. coordinate/subordinate structure change (. . . the body is sensitive to ordinary room light. And so frequently turning on a lamp . . . → . . . the body is sensitive to ordinary room light; therefore, frequently turning on a lamp . . .)

6. Here, as in all other lessons (except book reports), specialized vocabulary is provided before the reading to enable students to understand the terminology associated with the topic. It is not intended that the students learn or be tested on this vocabulary. It is there so that the students can conveniently read the article and get on with the purpose of the lesson.

7. Paraphrasing practices are important for two reasons. First, they give students practice in using context to guess the general meaning of a word or expression. The key words and phrases used in these practices were chosen because they are probably unfamiliar to many intermediate-to-advanced learners of English and because the contexts in which they occur provide good clues to their meaning. Secondly, the practices provide students with additional, more controlled paraphrasing experience. Again, our intention is not that these key words and expressions be learned and tested, but rather that the students recognize and perhaps eventually use them in their own writing.

8. The words in the Check Your Progress section here and throughout the text are those words from the reading(s) that are likely to be new to many students. They are offered as suggested additions to the students' own vocabulary lists. In preparing their vocabulary lists, students can select from among these or other words they feel will be valuable additions to their active vocabularies.

9. Suggest that students give rather short oral reports the first time they are assigned. If students have to speak for only 2 to 3 minutes, they feel less intimidated. Try to do Lesson B 3 before the next oral reports are to be given.

PART A, LESSON 3

1. Because of the variety of technology currently used in libraries in the United States (computer cataloging, microfiche, and so on), we have used a general approach to library use. You will have to adapt it to the library your students will be using.

2. If possible, arrange a library tour for your students. Some libraries, especially those at colleges, have a structured program to orient students to using the library. If such a program is not available, take your students to the library yourself. You may even want to spend a few class sessions there, helping the students to locate articles. You will find that with your help and the help of students who are more experienced in using the library, students become proficient quite quickly.

3. Point out that academic libraries usually do not subscribe to a large variety of popular magazines. Thus, many of the citations in

the *Readers' Guide* are not available. Students should learn to check whether the library carries a particular magazine and/or be directed to public libraries, where these are more readily found.

PART A, LESSON 4

1. We have included this lesson here because book reports are part of the course requirements, but it should probably be deferred until shortly before students must submit their first book report. We have found that at the beginning, students' need for practice in the other activities is greater than their need for this.

2. Demonstrating how to prepare a book report without actually having the students read the book is a difficult task. We were reluctant to assign a particular book because this contradicts the idea of "reading what you want to read." We attempted to solve this problem by (a) providing a rather lengthy summary of the Tannen book to demonstrate a nonfiction report, and (b) showing the video version of the Tyler book in class to demonstrate a fiction report. This seems to work. Of course, it is not necessary to do both.

   The Accidental Tourist is a charming film with simple dialog, which turns into a pleasurable experience for both students and teacher. It is also an interesting vehicle for discussion of American culture. The film is closed-captioned, and if the technology is available to you, showing it this way provides yet another reading experience in addition to helping students understand names and conversational usage.

3. We ask students to tell us beforehand which book they have chosen to read, usually in the first conference of the term. We suggest flexibility in determining the acceptability of their selections. If a student is a weak reader, we permit a simplified version of a novel. If a student has to read a longer, more complex book as a an assignment in an academic course, we permit a report on just part of that book. In other words, we try to make the book reports of equal complexity for all students because our goal is for them to enjoy the books and feel a sense of accomplishment in reading them.

PART B, LESSON 1

1. We strongly recommend that you do Practice 1 in class. The highlighting technique dramatically shows students how many words they *do* know. It also helps students realize that they don't have to be dependent on their dictionaries. Being able to answer the questions about the reading, despite not knowing all the words, reinforces this.

2. The number of words you ask students to include on their Reading Reports is up to you. We suggest two to five, but there will be times when students find only one or perhaps none in a particular article. The choice of which words they want to make part of their active vocabulary is up to them, although you may want to set a minimum total number of words to be learned each week.

3. Tell students they may choose a "specialized" word to add to their vocabulary list if they feel it will be helpful to them, but they should be encouraged to select other more high-frequency words.

PART B, LESSON 2

1. We tell students about the standard conventions for punctuation and capitalization of titles and ask that they use them when filling out the Reading Report Forms. If they are college students, they will need to know these rules eventually, and they may as well use them correctly from the start.

2. For your record-keeping purposes, insist that students check the proper place for "Type of Reading" on the report form.

3. Keep in mind that, unless yours is a combined reading/writing course, the Reading Reports should not be evaluated on the basis of writing skills. The purpose of these reports is to demonstrate the students' reading comprehension, and the reports themselves should not become an obstacle to enjoyment in reading. You and your students can decide to what extent errors in mechanics and usage will be corrected on the reports.

PART B, LESSON 3

1. We strongly urge you to do this lesson before the second round of oral reports and to use this topic for your first series of oral reports. Even skeptical students find the subject fascinating. This keeps the attention of the whole class, and in turn, encourages students whose oral skills are weak. Furthermore, because of the high interest in the topic, students ask questions to clarify what they are not able to understand, either because of pronunciation or poor organization in the report.

2. Again, because many academic libraries do not subscribe to popular magazines, tell students to use books or to go to public libraries to find their articles on this topic.

3. Use your discretion in determining the length of the oral reports. You may wish to begin with a 3 to 5 minute report and increase the length as the course progresses. Allow time for questions and discussion after each report.

4. We assign students to give a report on a particular day, but if there is a valid reason, we permit them to "trade" assigned dates if they notify us of the change.

5. If a student is absent on his or her report day and has an acceptable excuse, we try to fit the report in later. If there is no excuse, the student is not given credit for this assignment.

PART B, LESSON 4

1. Initially, group discussions tend to be unfocused, with students tending to merely summarize each reading. You will find that guidance is required. The teacher needs to float from group to group to keep students on the right track and to make sure that all are participating.

2. The composition of the group is critical to the success of this activity. Although groups are formed according to interest in the subject under discussion, try to encourage a mix of language groups and abilities. Also mix talkative students with quiet students. Groups will vary from week to week, so if you have a rather lackluster combination one week, you can be sure that it will change the following week.

3. We provide students with Group Report Forms as a guide for their discussions, but we are not particular about the way information is recorded on them. The forms should simply enable the reporter to tell the rest of the class what went on in the discussion. We do

not correct or return these forms, but we keep them in a separate file to serve as a record of what was discussed and who participated.

4. We did not originally plan to include debates as part of the course. However, because of the controversial nature of some topics, debates naturally evolved as another format for group discussion sessions. Our experience has been that it is better to wait until the independent reading phase of the course has been in place for a few weeks and the students have had some experience in group work before using the debate format. Debates may be organized on any controversial topic.

PART C, LESSON 1

1. This complex yet important lesson familiarizes students with the devices that writers use to influence their readers. If you plan to use the debate format in your class, it is a good idea to do this lesson before you begin the debates.

2. Many students have difficulty with the word choice section. We tell them, that if all else fails, to ask their native English-speaking friends. Although these same friends might have difficulty answering a question concerning English grammar, they will understand the connotation of words intuitively.

3. The treatment of logical fallacies here is admittedly superficial. Our intention is to introduce students to problems in logic and make them aware of how some writers attempt to manipulate thinking. We included these specific fallacies because they are common ones and because they happen to be in the readings.

4. Practice 4—Key: a. false dilemma (#3) b. conclusion based on little or no evidence (#4) c. personal attack (#2) d. one event necessarily leads to another event (#1)

5. Practice 5—Key: a. vocabulary 2. fact/opinion 3. vocabulary & logic (#1) 4. vocabulary 5. vocabulary and logic (#4) 6. vocabulary 7. vocabulary and fact/opinion 8. vocabulary and logic (#1) 9. logic (#5) 10. vocabulary and fact/opinion. 11. vocabulary and logic (#1) 12. vocabulary and logic (#1)

PART C, LESSON 2

1. Practice 2—Key: 1. having to convince people not to use drugs if they are legal 2. would increase; yes 3. unreliability of the quality of the drugs; illegality; high cost; increase in use 4. more frequent use would cost more money, leading to more crime 5. undercut the government price by selling on the black market 6. $10¢/gram; at 50¢/dose, even children could afford it

2. Using the debate format for group discussions is a particularly good experience in collaborative learning. We suggest allocating class time for the organizing and planning stages, including having the members of a team go to the library to locate information together.

3. The suggested format, while less formal than a true debate format, may be changed to something even more informal if that better suits your class. Likewise, the suggested timing (approximately one hour for each debate) can also be altered to whatever seems appropriate for your class.

4. You may want to devise point values and scoring sheets for the debates. Students not involved in a particular debate could then serve as "judges," and there would be a "winning" team.

5. We have videotaped some of our students' debates and showed them to the students later. While debating, students become so involved in the topic that they are not self-conscious about being taped. Watching their performance later becomes a confidence-builder.

PART C, LESSON 3

1. This supplemental activity is strictly optional. If you decide to do it, we suggest using it as a final, culminating activity. It is valuable in helping students deal with longer texts, and it also serves as an introduction to doing research.

2. If yours is a combined reading/writing course, you may wish to add your own materials on citing authority. We have not included any form of citation here because the readings are identified in the Reading Report and because we consider this a reading activity.

The Extensive Reading Course

Research studies have shown that students who read something because they are interested in it remember more of what they read and absorb more language.

Introduction

Reading on Your Own: An Extensive Reading Course may be unlike any reading book you have ever had. Up until now, you have probably had a reading textbook that provided you with selections you were supposed to read *intensively*. That is, you were asked to read the passages very carefully, looking up any unfamiliar vocabulary and making sure that you understood every word of the reading. You probably answered comprehension questions, did vocabulary exercises, and tried to "read between the lines" to interpret exactly what the author was saying. You may have also examined the reading selections for grammatical patterns that are typical of written English.

Most English as a Second (or Foreign) Language reading courses teach you how to read intensively. As a result, you may feel tied to your dictionary. You may be unable to read anything without looking up the words you do not know in your dictionary. You may believe that you cannot read books and magazines or even newspapers written for native speakers of English because you cannot understand all of the words. How could you possibly read a book? It would take forever to look up all the words you do not know.

This reading course and textbook are quite different. First of all, instead of reading intensively, you will now begin to read *extensively*. That is, you will read longer articles and try to get the main ideas the author is trying to communicate. You will not be expected to understand every word of what you read. Indeed, there may be times when you miss large sections of an article you are reading, but you should force yourself to continue reading; try to guess the meanings of unfamiliar words, and understand what you can. The emphasis will be on what you *can* understand, not what you cannot.

A second important difference is that this textbook will provide you with only a small fraction of your reading material. Most of what you read you will choose yourself. The purpose of this book is to help prepare you to read on your own by teaching you some strategies for reading longer selections written for native speakers of English, and by providing practice in using these strategies.

You will find that your confidence in your ability to read on your own will improve noticeably, due to the quantity of reading that you will do in this course. You will be asked to find and read two or three articles each week. These may come from a newspaper; a news magazine such as *Time*, *Newsweek*, or *U.S. News and World Report*; a popular magazine such as *People*, *Life*, *Reader's Digest*, or *Sports Illustrated*; a journal from an academic field; or even a chapter from a book. If you are taking an academic course in an American university, you may choose to use a section of a textbook or a journal article assigned for that class as one of your readings. Also, you will read at least one or two full-length books in English during this course. The books will be your choice, and they may be either fiction or nonfiction.

It is very important that you choose to read something that really interests you. Research studies have shown that students who read something because they are interested in it remember more of what they read and absorb more new language. You should vary your reading: choose some news articles and other selections on topics of special interest to you.

Overview of Course Requirements

In this lesson we give you an overview of the course requirements. In the next lesson, we will take you through each activity, and you will be given detailed instructions about what to do. Here are the major requirements of the course:

- **Reading Reports**

  Each week you will write a Reading Report on each of the articles you have read. First you will write a brief (one or two paragraph) summary of the main ideas of the article, and then you will give your response to what you have read. Did you agree or disagree with a point raised in the article? What opinions do you have on the topic you read about? A third part of your reading report is to create your own vocabulary list. An important benefit of reading is to increase your vocabulary, both the number of words you recognize and the number you learn to use. You are much more likely to remember and use words that you have chosen yourself, so as you read you will select several words from each reading to use for your personal vocabulary list. These words must be defined and used in sentences, and you will want to add them to your active vocabulary.

- **Oral Reports**

  Every week, or every other week, you will select one of your readings for an oral report to the class. At this time, you will stand up in front of the group and present an article that you think would interest your classmates. You will do an oral summary of the article, and then the class may wish to ask you questions, discuss the content, and offer opinions and additional information of their own.

- **Group Discussions and Reports**

  Each week you will participate in a small group discussion of a topic of interest to the group. Some weeks the groups will want to talk about questions that have arisen out of class discussions of the reading in the text, while other weeks the groups may choose to focus on an entirely new subject. In either case, group members will decide how to approach the topic, and then each person will go to the library and find an article on that subject. The next day all of the members of the group will report to the others on their article, and the group will then have an in-depth discussion of the topic. At the conclusion of their discussion, the members will prepare a group report and present it to the rest of the class.

- **Book Reports**
  For each book that you read, you will do a written and an oral book report. The written report will focus on the main ideas of the book and your response to it, and it will be about 500–600 words long. Your oral report will be about 10 or 15 minutes long and will give you an opportunity to share your book with your classmates. Some of them may choose to read your book if you liked it and you would recommend it. There will be detailed instructions on how to prepare your written book reports in Lesson 4.

Summary of Course Requirements

1. Prepare three Reading Reports with at least 10 vocabulary words per week, as assigned.
2. Do an oral report every week or every other week, as assigned.
3. Participate in weekly group discussions and group reports.
4. Prepare one or more book reports, as assigned.

Reading Strategies

One of the goals of this course is to teach you how to transfer the strategies you use in reading your native language over to reading English. Remember that when you read your native language, you read for different purposes. Sometimes you read very quickly to get an overview of the whole reading selection. Sometimes you are looking for a particular piece of information and when you find it, you read and study it very carefully. These are strategies that you need for reading English, too. Remember that in your native language you often skip over portions of an article that do not interest you. It is not necessary to understand or even read all of an article to gain some useful information from it.

As you read, you should look for the "big picture"—for the main ideas presented in the reading selection. Start by deciding what the article is about. Most of the time you will be able to do this by just reading the title of the article. We call the titles of articles in newspapers "headlines." Following are headlines from some newspaper articles. What do you think the topic is for each article?

With Shorter, Lighter Stories, Paper Seeks Younger Readers

Md. Considers 5% Sales Tax On Gasoline

Snow and Ice Storms Move Across Midwest

Street Fashion: Hats Incredible

A Winter Without Food

Talk of a famine forces Gorbachev to take action

MEDICINE
What twins tell us about schizophrenia

It's OK to Love Garlic Bread

Back to Basics After a Decade of Sophistication

Nevada's Pains Rooted in Growth

Nation's Fastest Census Gainer Sees More Congestion, Pollution

Massachusetts Police Have Few Clues in Sniper Killing

A new worry for microwave cooks

HEALTH ▪ Chemicals in plastic packaging may be leaking into our dinner

Football Playoff Opposition May Fade

Practice 1

Read the headlines and then decide which ones are on these topics:

the weather

an investigation of a murder

clothing

sports

problems in a fast-growing state

taxes

a newspaper

heredity and mental illness

problems in the Soviet Union

choosing simple food

problems with cooking food

When you read the newspaper in your native language, you read a headline, decide what the article is about, and then decide whether or not you are interested in reading about this subject.

Perhaps you are only interested in a certain aspect of the topic. You may decide to read the article quickly to find the answer to a specific question, for example. Or, you may read part of the article and then lose interest. Newspaper writers know this, and so in a straight news article, they put the most important information first. The information looks like an upside-down triangle, from most important to least important.

If you remember that straight news articles are arranged like this, you can concentrate more on understanding the beginning of the article, knowing that you will be getting the most important information there. You should note, however, that feature articles, columns, and editorials in newspapers do not follow this pattern of organization, nor do magazine articles.

Magazine articles and feature newspaper articles usually begin with interesting but non-essential information that is intended to attract the reader's attention. This may be an anecdote, a surprising or unusual fact, or virtually anything to get the reader to continue with the article. This introductory "attention-getter" can consist of one to four or five paragraphs, depending on the length of the article.

In one type of organization, the main idea of the text ordinarily follows the introduction, and the rest of the article consists of explanations, details and examples. Another kind of organization, sometimes used by writers who wish to persuade the reader to accept a particular point of view, is to follow the introductory section with a series of examples and details which lead the reader to the main idea in the very last part of the article. A newspaper editorial is an example of this type of persuasive writing.

When you are reading these types of articles, then, you cannot just read the beginning to get a general idea of what the article contains and assume that the information at the end is not important. If the writer is successful and makes you interested in the subject with the introduction, you will go on reading. Often you must finish the whole article to get the complete picture of what the point of the article is.

When you read a magazine article in your native language, you probably, at least occasionally, use a reading strategy called "previewing." That is, you take a quick look at the whole article to see how long it is and whether or not you want to read it. Previewing is an important strategy for you to use when selecting magazine articles to read for this class for two reasons: First, previewing will help you decide whether the article is really interesting to you and worth reading. Second, previewing will help you get an overview of what the article is about, and this will make it easier for you to pick up the main points of the reading.

When previewing a magazine article, you should read the title and the subtitle, look at the photographs, and read the captions written under them. If there are any charts or graphs in the article, you should look at those, too. All these illustrations can help you decide what the article is about and whether or not you are interested in reading it. Writers of longer articles frequently put in little headlines, or subheadings, to direct your attention to specific bits of information. By reading these subheadings, you can get a good overview of what the article is about.

Practice 2

Bring a newspaper into class. In small groups, read a number of headlines and guess what each article is about. Then, compare several articles and decide which ones are straight news articles and which ones are feature articles. Take turns reading aloud the opening sentence for several articles of both types. What do you notice? What do the feature articles use to get your attention? What strategies do you use to read straight news stories in your native language? What strategies do you use to read feature articles in your native language newspaper? How would you compare the newspapers in your country with those in the United States?

Practice 3

Bring a magazine to class. In small groups, preview several articles in each magazine by looking at photographs, illustrations, and graphs, and by reading subtitles, captions, and subheadings. What is each article about? What do you predict that you will learn in this article? What do you think the main idea of the article will be? What magazines do you enjoy reading in the United States? What kinds of magazines do you enjoy reading in your country?

Note that academic texts follow a third type of organization. In general, the introduction to a chapter in a textbook—one to several paragraphs—is a preview of the topics covered in the chapter. The rest of the reading consists of a discussion of each topic in the order announced in the introduction. The topics frequently have headings and subheadings to make the presentation easier to follow. Each discussion begins with a generalization about the topic, followed by detailed explanations and examples. Chapters commonly end with a summary section.

Because textbook writers are teachers, they tell you what they are going to say, they say it, and then they summarize what they have said. Therefore, when you are reading chapters in a textbook, you can determine the main idea by reading either the beginning or the end of the chapter. If you are interested in only one or two of the subjects, you can read the material in the sections with those subheadings, but if you need to thoroughly understand the subject matter, you must read the whole chapter.

Practice 4

In small groups, examine some textbooks your teacher has brought into class. Discuss the organization of the chapters. How do these texts compare to books you have used for courses in your country?

In summary, when reading an article in English, try to use a variety of strategies as you would when reading in your native language:

1. Decide what the article is about and whether you are interested in that topic.
2. Get an overview of the article by reading subtitles, subheadings, and captions and by looking at pictures and other illustrations. What is the main idea of this article?
3. Read through the article once without looking up any words, and get as much information as you can. Concentrate on the parts you find most interesting, and skip over parts that seem uninteresting or particularly difficult.
4. When you have finished, state the main idea of the article in your own words.

Can't get enough sleep? Read "Still Can't Sleep?" on page 12 to learn what advice the experts give.

Getting Started

In this lesson, you will learn how to do all the activities of the course, except how to do a book report, which is covered in Lesson 4.

- Participating in a small group discussion
- Writing a Reading Report: paraphrasing, summarizing, and creating your own vocabulary list
- Giving an oral report

Previewing a Reading

In the previous lesson, we discussed the importance of choosing an article on a subject that interests you and then previewing it to get an overview of what it is about. You will now read an article about getting a good night's sleep. As you read "Still Can't Sleep?", imagine that you have a friend who is having trouble sleeping at night. You see this article in a magazine and you know from the title that it has something to do with sleep. When you read the subtitle "Need more sleep but can't get it? Here are some suggestions," you know that this article will have suggestions for getting a good night's sleep. Perhaps you can get some ideas for your friend who has insomnia.

The subheadings at the beginning of each section summarize the author's suggestions, so you will want to read them first to get an overview of the article. Read the article now and be ready to state the main ideas presented in it. What advice will you be able to pass along to your friend?

Specialized Vocabulary You May Not Know

1. body clock or biological clock—the "clock" inside our bodies that tells us when it is time to go to sleep and when it is time to wake up

2. insomnia—not being able to fall asleep at night

3. nicotine—a chemical in tobacco that causes the heart to beat faster and may keep you awake

4. caffeine—a chemical found in drinks such as coffee, tea, and cola, and in chocolate that acts as a stimulant on the body and may keep you from being able to fall asleep

5. ephedrine—a chemical used in cold medicines that may keep you awake

Still Can't Sleep?   Need more sleep but can't get it? Here are some suggestions.

● **Stick to a regular sleep schedule.**
For unknown reasons, the body's daily rhythms follow a 25-hour cycle. What this means is that every day we must reset our body clocks to the earth's 24-hour day. Most people keep a regular schedule during the week, so the adjustment is only an hour and causes little inconvenience. On weekends, however, many of us follow our natural rhythms and stay up late, going to sleep an hour or so later on Friday night and two hours later on Saturday. By Sunday our bodies are two or three hours off schedule and come Monday morning we may feel logy and irritable. By keeping to a regular schedule as much as possible, your body clock won't have to work so hard to reset itself.

Workers on the night shift can reset their biological clocks by sleeping in total darkness during the day, and working under bright lights that simulate sunlight, rather than conventional indoor lighting.

● **Get regular vigorous exercise.**
By relaxing muscles and stimulating the release of endorphins—chemicals that act as natural pain relievers—exercise works as an antidote to stress. It can help you fall asleep more quickly and sleep more soundly. Schedule exercise no later than early evening, since strenuous activity too close to bedtime can stimulate.

● **Watch your diet.**
There are no magic sleep foods, but a meal schedule, just like a steady sleep schedule, helps keep your body clock running smoothly. Eating too late in the evening, especially heavy or spicy foods, can keep you awake, since digestion can delay sleep, cautions Michael J. Thorpy, M.D., director of the Sleep-Wake Disorders Cen-

ter at Montefiore Hospital in New York. And because hunger can keep you awake, dieters should save a few calories for a light before-bed snack. Beware of middle-of-the-night snacking. You might train your body to wake up for food!

● **Be wary of sleeping pills.**
They may leave you as groggy as a poor night's sleep. And if you rely on pills to help you sleep, you may find your insomnia is even worse when you try to sleep without them. You can also develop a tolerance; after a while they lose their effectiveness and you need larger doses or stronger drugs.

Some people have found that the amino acid L-tryptophan is an effective sleep aid, but supplements recently have been associated with a potentially fatal blood disorder known as eosino-philia-myalgia syndrome (EMS). Currently, the FDA advises discarding all L-tryptophan on your shelves.

● **Avoid stimulants near bedtime.**
These include the nicotine in cigarettes, the caffeine in coffee, tea, chocolate, colas and diet pills, and cold remedies containing ephedrine.

● **Limit late-evening alcohol.**
A drink may help you fall asleep, but you probably won't get a good night's rest. Alcohol suppresses restorative dream sleep, causes numerous short awakenings and, once its sedative effects have worn off, may leave you wide awake but unrefreshed toward morning.

● **Relax before bedtime.**
You need at least an hour to unwind. Read a book, listen to quiet music, take a hot

bath or try relaxation techniques, such as meditation or yoga.

● **Leave the lights off if you wake up in the middle of the night.**
New research suggests that several hours of light absorbed through the eyes can actually reset our biological clocks, reports Charles Czeisler, M.D., director of Circadian and Sleep Disorder Medicine at Brigham and Women's Hospital in Boston. The researchers used bright light comparable in intensity to natural sunlight just after dawn (at least 100 times stronger than ordinary room light), which reset subjects' body clocks by as much as 12 hours and made them as alert at midnight as they would ordinarily be at noon. But the study also found that the body is sensitive to ordinary room light as well. And so frequently turning on a lamp to read in the middle of the night could affect your internal clock and aggravate your sleep problems.

● **Really can't sleep?**
If you're drifting in and out of sleep, Thorpy advises staying in bed. "You'll get some rest that way." And though easier said than done, try not to worry about it. Insomnia won't last forever. When your body really needs to sleep, it will.

If insomnia still plagues you, write to the American Sleep Disorders Association, 604 Second St. SW, Rochester, MN 55902. The association will send a free information packet, consisting of brochures about sleep and a list of 140 sleep-disorders centers across the country. You can also ask them specific sleep questions.

Reprinted from "Still Can't Sleep?," *McCall's*, August 1990, 46.

Participating in a Small Group Discussion

In this course, you will frequently be asked to discuss reading selections in small groups of students. When you form your small group, choose a leader and a reporter. The leader will make sure that the group stays on the topic, answers all the questions, and does any other assigned tasks. The leader will also make sure that everyone has a chance to express his or her opinion and that no one dominates the conversation. The reporter will take notes on the discussion and then will tell the rest of the class about it at the end of the class hour.

Each lesson in this book contains at least one reading selection. After the reading there are Questions for Discussion. You should get into small groups, answer the questions, and discuss any other aspects of the topic that interest you. This is also the time to help each other with any parts of the reading that may have been difficult to understand.

In Lesson 3 you will learn how to find articles on specific topics in the library. You will form small groups to choose topics to research, find articles and read them, and then have a discussion with other members of your small group. Your teacher will probably ask your group to prepare a written report of your discussion, and for that you will use the small Group Discussion Report Form found on page 21.

Questions for Discussion

1. Have you ever experienced jet lag when traveling to a foreign country? How did you feel? How did it affect your sleeping? How long did it take to reset your biological time clock?

2. What do you do to relax before going to bed at night?

3. Do you ever have trouble sleeping? What do you do when you can't sleep? How much sleep do you usually get each night?

4. Are you a morning person or a night person? How does this affect the way you live? Does it cause problems with the people you live with?

5. What do you think about the advice in "Still Can't Sleep?" Does caffeine keep you awake? Do you have a different sleeping schedule on the weekends?

A Word about Vocabulary

In this book we will treat vocabulary in three different ways:

1. Specialized vocabulary
2. Paraphrasing useful words and phrases
3. Check your progress: words you should know or add to your personal vocabulary list

First, just before the beginning of the reading selection, we list words that we consider to be specialized vocabulary. These words are defined for you, and they are provided to help you get through the article with ease. In some cases the words are so specialized to that topic that you may never see them again unless you do further reading on that subject. In many cases these words have a rather narrow meaning, and although you need to be able to recognize them as you read, you are not likely to make them part of your active vocabulary. In this lesson, we have chosen these words and phrases as specialized vocabulary: body clock or biological clock, insomnia, nicotine, caffeine, and ephedrine.

A second list is made up of sentences containing words that have more general use and should be added to your active vocabulary so that you can use them in your own speaking and writing. We have chosen these words not only because they are useful for you to know, but also because the words surrounding them give enough information for you to be able to guess their meaning. The information surrounding a word is called "context." It is important for you to use context when you read in order to guess at the meanings of words, instead of taking time to look them up in the dictionary. Sometimes the context will actually provide you with a definition of the word, as in this sentence taken from the article you just read:

> "By relaxing muscles and stimulating the release of **endorphins**—chemicals that act as natural pain relievers—exercise works as an antidote to stress."

The word *endorphins* is clearly defined as "chemicals that act as natural pain relievers." In most cases, however, you will have to figure out the meaning of an unfamiliar word for yourself using information found in the context. For example, what do you guess is the meaning of the word *simulate* in the following sentence:

> "Workers on the night shift can reset their biological clocks by sleeping in total darkness during the day, and working under bright lights that **simulate** sunlight, rather than conventional indoor lighting."

If you were to write the phrase "bright lights that simulate sunlight" in your own words, you might write something like "bright lights that are similar to sunlight" or "are like sunlight." The idea of the sentence is that people who work at night can fool their body clocks into believing that it is daytime by working under lights that are bright like the sun.

Restating something in your own words is called "paraphrasing." It is something you do in your native language without much thought, and it is an important skill for you to have in English, also. When you write about what you have read, for example, you will have to paraphrase; you must not copy sentences directly from the reading selection. In order to give you practice in doing this, as well as in using context clues to guess the meanings of unfamiliar words, you will be asked to paraphrase some sentences or phrases from the reading selection.

Practice 1

The following sentences contain key words and phrases from the reading. Paraphrase the parts indicated to show that you understand their meaning. Try to do this practice without using a dictionary.

EXAMPLE: "And if you **rely on** pills to help you sleep, you may find your insomnia is even worse when you try to sleep without them."

Paraphrased answer: You should not **depend on** sleeping pills to help you fall asleep.

1. "You can also *develop a **tolerance***; after a while they lose their effectiveness and you need larger doses or stronger drugs."
2. "*Be **wary** of sleeping pills.* They may leave you as groggy as a poor night's sleep."
3. "A drink may help you fall asleep, but you probably won't get a good night's rest. Alcohol, . . . once its ***sedative** effects* have worn off, may leave you wide awake but unrefreshed toward morning."
4. "Leave the lights off if you wake up in the middle of the night. New research suggests that several hours of *light **absorbed** through the eyes* can actually reset our biological clocks. . . . "
5. "And so frequently turning on a lamp to read in the middle of the night could affect your internal clock and ***aggravate** your sleep problems.*"

The third type of vocabulary list you will find in this text (Check Your Progress) is a list of words from the reading that you should at least learn to recognize in your independent reading. These are words that are used frequently in writing, and as you advance in your ability to write English, they really should become part of your active vocabulary. If there are any words on this list you do not know, you may wish to use some of them for your personal vocabulary list.

Check Your Progress

Look at the following useful words from the reading. If there are any you don't recognize or know how to use, consider selecting them to add to your vocabulary list:

schedule	stimulate	antidote	comparable
irritable	stress	discard	sensitive

Each week you will create your own vocabulary list of words taken from articles you have read. You will choose these words on your own, write the sentence in which you found the word, indicate its part of speech, give a brief definition, and use it in a sentence to show that you clearly understand the meaning of the word and how to use it. For example:

"By Sunday our bodies are two or three hours off schedule and come Monday morning we may feel **logy** and irritable."

logy—adjective; heavy or dull, especially in motion or thought

After taking all that medicine, when I was finally able to get up, I felt **logy**, and I had a hard time thinking clearly.

Summarizing and Paraphrasing the Main Ideas of a Reading

When you tell someone about something you have read in your native language, you use your own words. Most of the time you do not have the book or article in front of you as you talk. You summarize what the author has said, focusing on what you found interesting, and you paraphrase as you speak. In this course, you will share articles you read with your classmates and, of course, you will tell about them in your own words. Sometimes this will be done in small discussion groups, and sometimes you will make oral reports to the entire class. You will also need to summarize and paraphrase the main ideas of articles you have read when you write your Reading Reports each week.

In "Still Can't Sleep?" the author offers nine suggestions for getting a good night's sleep. Each suggestion is printed in bold face type as a subheading, dividing the reading into sections. If you were telling someone about this article, you would summarize and paraphrase at the same time. For example, in the first section the author advises us to establish a regular time to go to bed each night. Because our bodies are on a 25-hour cycle and our days are 24 hours long, we may have a tendency to stay up later on weekends and throw our biological time clocks off. It is therefore easier to fall asleep if we go to bed at the same time every night.

Practice 2

In small groups, summarize and paraphrase the rest of the article in the same way. Have one member of the group write down the information for each point. You should have eight or nine sentences to express the eight remaining pieces of advice. When you have finished, share your papers with another group and compare how you summarized and paraphrased the information.

Writing a Reading Report

Each week you will choose two or three articles from newspapers or magazines, read them and write a Reading Report for each one using the Reading Report Form found on page 20. First, you will write your name and the date at the top of the form, and then you will complete the information about the article. Here is the information about the reading you have just completed.

Title: "Still Can't Sleep?"

Author: none

Type of Magazine: Popular

Name of Publication: *McCall's*

Date of Article or Book: August 1990

Number of Pages: 1

Type of Reading: Group (class assignment)

Next, you will write a one or two paragraph summary of the reading, being careful to paraphrase; do not copy any sentences directly. The first sentence of your summary should state the main idea of the reading, e.g., "This article offers practical tips on how to overcome insomnia." After summarizing the main points, you will write your response to the article. What is your opinion about this subject? Did you agree or disagree with any of the author's statements? Finally, on the back of the Reading Report Form, you will list three or four vocabulary words, writing the sentence (or a part of it, if it is very long) where you found the word, the part of speech, the definition, and your original sentence that you write to show you know how to use the word correctly.

Summary for "Still Can't Sleep?"

This article offers practical tips on how to overcome insomnia. First, we should establish a regular time to go to bed each night. Because our bodies are on a 25-hour cycle and our days are 24 hours long, we may have a tendency to stay up later on weekends and throw our biological time clocks off. It is therefore easier to fall asleep if we go to bed at the same time every night. Other suggestions for getting a good night's sleep include: exercise regularly, avoid eating heavy or spicy foods late at night, stay away from sleeping pills, avoid stimulants such as cigarettes and drinks with caffeine near bedtime, don't drink too much alcohol, and take time to unwind before going to bed. If you still have trouble sleeping and you wake up during the night, don't turn on the lights. Just relax and don't worry about not sleeping. Your body will let you sleep when you get tired enough.

RESPONSE   I found this article very interesting. Although much of the advice is common sense and reflects good health habits in general, there were some surprises. I did not know, for instance, that our body clocks are on a 25-hour cycle and that we have to reset them every day. Also, the article talked about light being absorbed through our eyes and having the side effect of changing our internal clock.

Practice 3

Practice your paraphrasing and summarizing skills by reading the following paragraphs and writing a one-sentence summary of each one.

Now it's official. Women who work outside the home average 20 to 25 *fewer* minutes of sleep a night than their male counterparts, who are getting somewhere between seven and eight hours a night.

Nothing Wrong With a Nap

Sleep experts have also given the nod to the nap. A quick snooze will sharpen your concentration and decision-making ability—and improve your mood and energy level—especially if you didn't get enough sleep the night before. Nappers often find that they are actually more productive overall than if they hadn't napped.

Nobody can figure out why we need two kinds of sleep: Rapid Eye Movement (REM) sleep, during which the eyes dart rapidly, and non-REM sleep, which includes light sleep or drowsiness, intermediate sleep and ultimately deep sleep.

Most dreaming occurs during REM sleep. Richard Coleman, a California sleep researcher, has said that the brain works like a computer, in which files are reorganized, updated and erased; REM sleep may be the way the brain handles housekeeping. It would be difficult to update our memory bank while we were awake and functioning, Coleman says.

Aside from being drowsy at night, there's another time when we become tired: midafternoon. Regardless of whether people have slept enough the night before—and regardless of how much they ate for lunch—this midday dip in alertness usually hits about 12 hours after the middle of nighttime sleep, according to Scott Campbell of the Institute of Circadian Physiology in Boston. In other words, if you sleep from 11 P.M. to 7 A.M. the urge to nap would hit around 3 P.M. With the exception of early birds and night owls—who make up less than 10 percent of the population—most people follow this daily cycle.

Reprinted from *The Washington Post*, 30 October 1990, and from "Still Can't Sleep?," *McCall's*, August 1990, 46.

Practice 4

Select an article from a newspaper or magazine, read it, decide what the main ideas are, and bring it to class. Form small groups, and make an oral report about your article to other members of the group. Do not be tempted to read from your article. Put it aside and tell about it in your own words. Your report should take about five to ten minutes. Share your reaction to the article with the other group members, and then discuss any aspect of this reading that interests the group. Be sure that everyone has a chance to speak.

Tips on Making a Good Oral Report

1. Keep it simple. Don't try to tell everything in the article.
2. Make it interesting.
3. Make eye contact with the people you are talking to.
4. Start with a good introduction. Tell them what the article is about before you begin.
5. Explain the main points clearly.
6. End with a good conclusion. Tell what you found interesting about the article. Give your opinion. Ask others what they think.

Practice 5

Write a Reading Report on the article you have just shared with the group. Use the Reading Report Form on page 20. Be sure to fill in all the information at the top of the form, then write your summary of the article. State the main idea in the first sentence of the summary, and make certain that you paraphrase the information you give; do not copy sentences from the reading. Finally, write your response to the article, and on the back of the Reading Report Form, start your personal vocabulary list. Remember to write the sentence where you found the word, the part of speech, and the definition. Then, make up your own sentence to show that you understand how to use it.

Topics for Further Investigation

1. Dreams
2. Research on sleep
3. Insomnia
4. Jet lag
5. Chronic fatigue syndrome
6. Circadian rhythms

Name _____

Date _____

READING REPORT

Title _____   Author _____

Name of Publication _____   Number of Pages _____

Date of Publication _____

Type of Reading: _____ Group _____ Personal Interest _____ Academic/Serious

Source of Reading: _____ Chapter in a Book

                    _____ Newspaper Article

                    _____ Magazine Type: _____ News _____ Popular _____ Serious

                    _____ Journal Article

                    _____ Other _____

SUMMARY

RESPONSE

VOCABULARY

GROUP DISCUSSION REPORT FORM

Names of Students   Names of Articles

_____

_____

_____

_____

_____

Summary of Discussion:

Questions Raised:

How long would you want to be
kept alive by machines? "End
Game" on pages 30 and 31 discusses
this complicated issue.

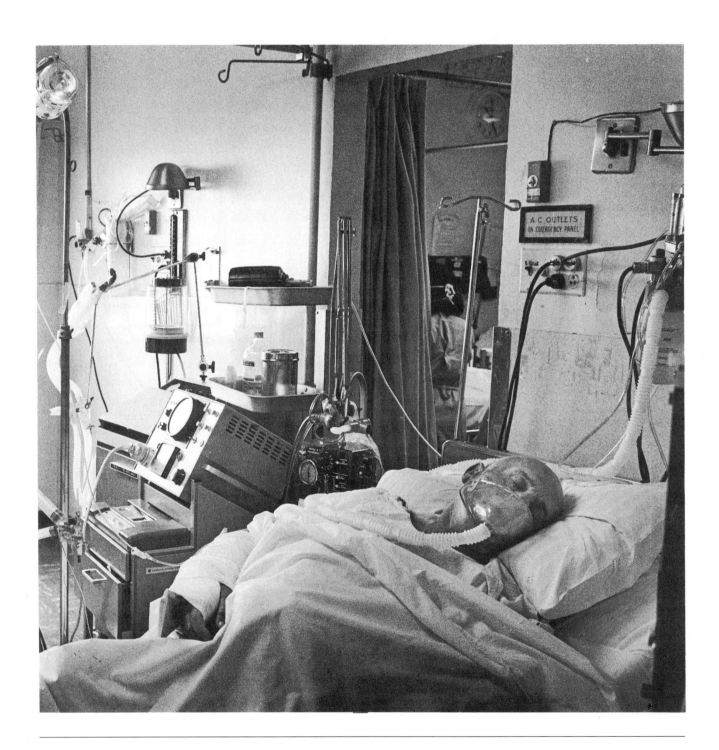

Selecting and Locating Readings

Much of the enjoyment of reading comes from learning more about interesting topics. You can easily find articles of interest by scanning a newspaper or magazine. This is the kind of reading you might do on an airplane or bus. More frequently, however, you are interested in a particular topic, or perhaps you have to write a report about it for a class, so you need to find articles about the subject. Obviously, it is not efficient to look randomly through magazines for articles on your topic. A better method of finding readings on a specific subject is to use the library. Your library can provide you with reading material from magazines, newspapers, and books on any subject that interests you.

Academic and Public Libraries

There are two types of libraries in the United States: university libraries, which subscribe to magazines and journals dealing with academic topics, and public libraries, which subscribe to popular magazines dealing with topics that appeal to the general public. If you are interested in finding an article about computer applications for accounting, for instance, a university library would be more likely to have a variety of articles than a public library would. If you wanted to find an article about the most recent World Cup matches, however, a public library would have more magazines that include articles about sports. For this reason, you may have to use your local public library to find some of the readings for this course. Such libraries are free, and anyone can use the materials in them. If you want to check out library books, records, or videos, you can easily get a library card. Newspapers, magazines, journals, and other reference materials cannot be checked out. You must use them in the library.

Finding Books in the Library

Your library is a rich resource for books on the subject you choose. All libraries arrange books according to their subject matter, using a cataloging system. Academic libraries generally use the Library of Congress system, while public libraries may use the Dewey Decimal System. No matter which system is used, each book in the library will be listed at least three times in the catalog: by title, author(s), and subject(s). You will be searching for books by using their subject entries in the cataloging system.

In the past, all libraries had a catalog system where each book had a separate card filed alphabetically in drawers for each of its three (at least) entries. Although some libraries still use a card catalog, modern technology has enabled libraries to categorize their books more efficiently. Now some libraries use a microfiche method for cataloging books, and others use computer systems. If your library has a computer system, you will find that it requires no technical skill to learn and that it makes finding books on a particular subject very easy.

The catalog, whether it is in printed form (cards), on microfiche, or on a computer, is divided into three broad categories: title, author, and subject. In all cases, the title entry, the author entry, and the subject entry for each book in the library are separately listed. If there are cards, each category is filed alphabetically in separate sets of drawers. If there is microfiche, each film is kept on separate film panels, listed in alphabetical order. If there is a computer system, special words or symbols are used to access an entry.

Whichever system your library uses, they all provide the same basic information you need to find a book on your subject. Each book is assigned a special number which serves as its "address" in the library. This number is known as the call number and actually consists of a series of numbers and letters. Books are placed on shelves in the library according to the number assigned to them.

When you have located the book you wish to find in the catalog, write down its title, its author, and its call number (be sure to write everything!). If your library has "open stacks," go to the shelf which has the number you are looking for. It may take you a while to learn your way around the library, but you will find that very soon you will become an expert! If your library has a "closed stack" system, fill out a request form for the book, and a library clerk will bring it to you.

Finding Articles in Periodicals

You will be able to find articles from magazines and newspapers by using a periodicals index. A periodicals index lists articles published in magazines, journals, and newspapers according to topic. The most general of these indexes is *The Readers' Guide to Periodical Literature*, which lists articles published in popular magazines. Most major newspapers, such as the *Los Angeles Times* and the *Washington Post*, publish an index of the articles in their own newspapers as well. In addition, there are many specialized indexes: *Business Periodicals Index*, *The Humanities Index*, and *The Public Affairs Information Service* list articles published in academic journals within specific fields. If you want to find articles about a subject in a particular academic discipline, ask a librarian which ones to use.

In this course, you will be reading articles on general subjects rather than academic ones, for the most part. Therefore, you will be using the *Readers' Guide*, as it is commonly known, and various newspaper indexes to find your articles. Learning how to use *The Readers' Guide* will, however, enable you to use any of the other indexes, since they all function in basically the same way.

Indexes are available in any library, either in the periodicals room or in the reference room. They are updated regularly, with an annual edition published at the end of each year. Articles are listed in alphabetical order by subject and author. Indexes also include such helpful information as subheadings and suggestions for other topic headings on similar subjects.

Following is a page taken from a monthly edition of the *Readers' Guide*.

READERS' GUIDE TO PERIODICAL LITERATURE

Subject Heading ➡

RIGHT OF PRIVACY—*cont.*
Great Britain
Private life and the public eye. J. Fenby. il *The Unesco Courier* 43:20-3 S '90
RIGHT OF PROPERTY
Germany (East)
Whose house is this anyway? B. Rudolph. il *Time* 136:78 Jl 9 '90
RIGHT TO DIE
See also

Other headings with articles on ➡ the same topic

Euthanasia
Living wills
National Council for Death and Dying

Changing the rules on dying [Supreme Court rules on N. Cruzan case] T. Gest. il *U.S. News & World Report* 109:22+ Jl 9 '90
End game. J. Poppy. il *Esquire* 114:75-6 Ag '90
Extraordinary means. J. Garvey. *Commonweal* 117:443-4 Ag 10 '90
The family vs. the state [Supreme Court decides N. Cruzan case] D. A. Kaplan. il *Newsweek* 116:22-3 Jl 9 '90
Has the 'right to die' arrived? K. A. Lawton. il *Christianity Today* 34:38-9 Ag 20 '90
Life and death questions [discussion of March 1990 article, Death with dignity & the sanctity of life] L. Kass. *Commentary* 90:2+ Ag '90
A limited right to die [Supreme Court decision in N. Cruzan case] O. Friedrich. il por *Time* 136:59 Jl 9 '90
Lord of mercy and compassion. H. Fehren. *U.S. Catholic* 55:39-41 Ag '90
Quinn's sins [discussion of May 4, 1990 article, When should the state step aside? Three views of the Cruzan case: issues and ramifications] *Commonweal* 117:402+ Jl 13 '90
The right to die in dignity. M. Angell. por *Newsweek* 116:9 Jl 23 '90
The suicide machine. D. Neff. il *Christianity Today* 34:14 Ag 20 '90
RIGHT TO LIFE MOVEMENT *See* Prolife movement
RIGHTS, CIVIL *See* Civil rights
RIGHTS OF EMPLOYEES *See* Employees—Civil rights

Author Heading ➡ **RIHA, JOHN**
Burn this. il *Esquire* 114:64 S '90
RIKERS ISLAND PRISON (NEW YORK, N.Y.) *See* New York (N.Y.)—Prisons
RILEY, PAT
about
Pat Riley. M. Murphy. por *TV Guide* 38:10 S 29-O 5 '90
RINALDI, DOMENIC
about
Family harvest. W. B. Logan. il por *House & Garden* 162:68+ S '90
RINCON, ANTONIO, D. 1541
about
Fatal diplomacy, 1541. L. Frey and M. Frey. bibl f il pors map *History Today* 40:10-15 Ag '90
RINFRET, PIERRE
about
The sound and the fury. R. E. Tyrrell. il *The American Spectator* 23:8 Ag '90
RING GALAXIES *See* Galaxies
RING OF FIRE AQUARIUM (OSAKA, JAPAN)
An experience of captivity. J. Adler. il *Newsweek* 116:50-1 Jl 30 '90
RING SYSTEMS (ASTRONOMY)
See also
Saturn (Planet)—Ring system
RING UM DEN RING [ballet] *See* Ballet reviews—Single works
RINGOEN, RICHARD
about
From glass jars to Star Wars and back again. K. Kelly, il *Business Week* p62-3 Ag 20 '90
RINGS
A familiar ring [son wears father's old ring] B. Brower, il *The New York Times Magazine* p14+ Jl 22 '90
RINGS OF TREES *See* Tree rings
RIO, DONALD C.
(jt. auth) *See* Siebel, Christian W., and Rio, Donald C.
RIO DE JANEIRO (BRAZIL)

Subheading ➡ **Monuments, statues, etc.**
On high [restoring Christ the Redeemer statue] B. Weber. il *The New York Times Magazine* p46 Jl 22 '90

RIOJA, PILAR
about
Reviews:
Performances by P. Rioja. D. Hering. por *Dance Magazine* 64:78-9 S '90
RIORDAN, RICHARD
about
Getting the politicians off their . . . J. H. Taylor. il pors *Forbes* 146:104-6 O 1 '90
RIORDAN FOUNDATION
Getting the politicians off their . . . J. H. Taylor. il pors *Forbes* 146:104-6 O 1 '90
RIOS, ALBERTO
The influenzas [poem] *The New Yorker* 66:48 S 10 '90
RIOS, MIGUEL ANGEL
about
Miguel Angel Rios at Baghoomian. F. T. Castle. *Art in America* 78:170 Jl '90
RIOTS
California
See also
Watts (Los Angeles, Calif.)—Riot, 1965
Kenya
See also
Nairobi (Kenya)—Riots
Romania
See also
Bucharest (Romania)—Riots
South Africa
Black on black bloodbath [Inkatha vs. African National Congress] J. Contreras and J. Whitmore. il *Newsweek* 116:41-2 Ag 27 '90
Blunting the spear [peace talks and bloodshed] S. MacLeod. il *Time* 136:52 Ag 20 '90
Challenge to the A.N.C. [tribal violence during ceasefire] *The Nation* 251:257 S 17 '90
Cracking heads in South Africa [police brutality] J. Contreras. il *Newsweek* 116:43 S 17 '90
Peaceful talk, violent acts. J. Contreras. il *Newsweek* 116:49 Ag 20 '90
Roar of the lions [tribal violence splits African National Congress and Inkatha] G. Garcia. il *Time* 136:43-4 Ag 27 '90
Says Mandela and Buthelezi should meet to help halt slaying of blacks by blacks. il pors *Jet* 78:12 O 1 '90
South Africa's crackdown. J. Contreras. il *Newsweek* 116:49 S 3 '90
A spreading tribal war. M. Nemeth. il *Maclean's* 103:27 S 3 '90
The tribal factor. *The New Republic* 203:7-8 O 1 '90
Turning point for Pretoria? J. Contreras. il *Newsweek* 116:34-5 O 1 '90
RIPOFFS *See* Fraud
RIPPE, JAMES M.
Staying loose. il *Modern Maturity* 33:72+ Je/Jl '90
RISBOURG, PASCALE
about
Pascale Risbourg. C. Carter. il por *Vogue* 180:142 Ag '90
RISC *See* Reduced instruction set computers
RISK
Real risks. J. W. Merline. *Consumers' Research Magazine* 73:38 Ag '90
What, me worry? [health risks; cover story] C. Russell. il *American Health* 9:44-51 Je '90
Anecdotes, facetiae, satire, etc.
The new puritanism. D. E. Koshland, Jr. *Science* 248:1057 Je 1 '90
RISK MANAGEMENT
The rewards of risk management. J. E. Bahls. il *Nation's Business* 78:58+ S '90
What's wrong with this picture? [credit risk and the banking system] A. G. Shilling. il *Forbes* 146:62-3 Ag 6 '90
RISK TAKING (PSYCHOLOGY)
Figure out how much risk you can take [investments] L. N. Vreeland. *Money* 19:26 S '90
Taking risks. P. J. Ryan. *America* 163:47 Jl 14-21 '90
Those thrills and chills: how you love 'em! W. Woodward. il *Teen* 34:49+ Je '90
RITCHIE, CEDRIC
about
Cedric Ritchie. P. Chisholm. por *Maclean's* 103:31 Jl 30 '90
RITES AND CEREMONIES
See also
Altars
Circumcision
Indians of South America—Rites and ceremonies

Suppose that you wish to find an article on the ethics of keeping a terminally ill or comatose person alive through modern medical technology. Articles on this subject can be found under the subject listing of "Right to Die." Notice that the subject (and author) headings appear in bold print and capital letters at the left margin. Immediately beneath the subject heading you will find "See also" if this topic is listed under other subject headings. In this case, you could look under the subject headings "Euthanasia," "Living wills," or "National Council for Death and Dying" for other articles on the same topic.

Each entry gives you the information you need to find that article in the periodicals section of the library. As you will notice, the entry (or listing) for each article is not easy to interpret, primarily because many abbreviations are used, particularly in *Readers' Guides* published before 1989, where even the magazine titles are abbreviated. At the beginning or end of these indexes, you will find a list of the abbreviations and their meanings. At first, you will have to consult the list frequently to understand an entry. As you continue to use the index, you will become familiar with the common ones and will be less dependent on this list. You should also be aware that normal conventions of capitalization and punctuation are not followed, another factor which sometimes makes it difficult to interpret the entries.

Let us examine and interpret one of the entries.

End game. J. Poppy. il *Esquire* 114:75-6 Ag '90
   (1)   (2)   (3) (4)   (5) (6)   (7)

1. The complete title of the article, followed by a period. Only the first letter is capitalized.
2. The author, followed by a period. The initial letter of the author's given name appears first, followed by the full family name.
3. An abbreviation to let you know the article includes an illustration.
4. The name of the magazine.
5. The volume number of the magazine.
6. The pages on which you will find the article.
7. The date of publication with an abbreviation for August (Ag).

It is important to copy all the information from the entry if you decide you want to read the article. In some cases, the volume number may not be needed, but it is better to establish the habit of copying all the information.

After examining the entry for "End Game," you now know that you must find the August, 1990, issue of *Esquire* magazine. Your first stop should be the serials list. This is a list (usually a computer print-out) of the magazines available in that library. The list includes the name of the magazine, the issues which the library has by date, and the location of the magazine. If the name or date of the magazine is not in the serials list, it means that the library does not have what you are looking for. Not all libraries use the same words and symbols in their serials list, but the following example will give you an idea of what a listing will tell you about the availability of a magazine.

```
Serials List                                    Page 26
          T I T L E

ESPRIT CREATEUR, L'
Location: Periodicals          Call No. 00000
Holdings:  Vol. 1 (1961) - Vol. 29 (1989)

L'ESPRIT NOUVEAU
Location: Stacks               Call No. NX 2 E8
Holdings:  Vol. 1 (1920) - Vol. 28 (1925)

ESQUIRE
Location: Periodicals          Call No. 00000
Holdings:  March 1967 - Dec. 1991

  Note: Current issues also in Periodicals Reading Room

ESSAY AND GENERAL LITERATURE INDEX
Location: Reference Room       Call No. RI/AI 3
Holdings:  Vol. 1 (1900-33) - Vol. 10 (1980-84)
```

Esquire is the third item on the list. After "Holdings," you can see that this library has all of the issues of this magazine from March, 1967 through December, 1991. You also know that these and the current issues, as well as the older ones, are in the periodicals reading room of this library.

All libraries keep periodicals in a separate section. If you are looking for an article in a current magazine or newspaper—dated within two to three months of the time you are looking for it—ask for it at the periodicals desk. Current issues are kept there. Older issues are bound together like a book, usually by year of publication.

If your library has open stacks, go to the periodicals section and look for the bound copies of the magazine, which will be arranged alphabetically on shelves. When you have located the bound copies of *Esquire*, look for the volume that contains the 1990 issues. If your library has closed stacks, fill out a request form for the August, 1990 issue. Within the volume, find the August issue and turn to page 75.

All periodical indexes work in the same way, although sometimes all but the most recent newspapers and some magazines are on microfilm rather than in bound copies. If this is the case, you can read and even make photocopies of your article on a microfilm reader in the microfilm section of the library.

Read the following article found from this entry.

SPECIALIZED VOCABULARY

1. life-sustaining—any treatment (medicine or machines) that is necessary for a patient to continue to live

2. CPR (cardiopulmonary resuscitation)—a procedure involving pounding on the chest of a person whose heart has stopped beating to restore the heartbeat

3. dialysis—a procedure which removes impure substances from a person's kidney to enable the organ to continue to function

4. tube-feeding—providing a person nutrients in liquid form by injection in order to continue life

5. irreversible coma—a state of permanent unconsciousness caused by disease or injury

6. trauma team—doctors and nurses who, under emergency conditions, treat a patient who has a severe injury that causes the body to go into shock and body organs to function at a low level

7. pediatric—dealing with the medical care and treatment of infants and children

8. in extremis—at the point of death

9. intensive care unit (also known as ICU)—the part of a hospital that cares for patients whose condition is so serious that they require constant attention

10. paramedic—a trained medical assistant (not a doctor or a nurse) who works in a rescue vehicle to provide immediate, emergency medical help

11. subdural hematoma—a swelling filled with blood in the brain

12. hemorrhage—heavy bleeding

13. pneumonia—a serious infection of the lungs causing them to fill with fluid and making breathing difficult

14. neurosurgeon—a medical doctor who treats the nervous system, including the brain and the spinal cord

15. living will—a legal document that specifies what medical treatment a person wants to receive if he or she becomes unable to communicate

16. durable power—a legal document that appoints another person to make decisions about medical treatment for a person who becomes unable to communicate

17. power of attorney—a legal document that appoints another person to handle all legal matters for a person

End Game   By John Poppy

WHEN ARE YOU GOING to get to it?'' I ask myself as I put off the decision for another day.

I'll start a list—in an intensive-care unit, these good intentions can fall apart unless they're explicit: "If I become unable to make health-care decisions for myself, I want life-sustaining treatment continued as long as both my physicians and my appointed agent believe the expected benefits of treatment will outweigh the expected burdens. On the other hand, I want such treatment terminated if. . . ."

But every start opens the prospect of a labor I'd rather not face. The questions, the questions. Which "life-sustaining" treatments—CPR, mechanical ventilation, surgery, dialysis, drugs? What else? Tube-feeding? What "benefits"? Can I really know in advance which elements of life will seem precious enough to keep above the line? Which "burdens"—poverty, pain, lost body parts? Heroes live with all of those, but who knows what I'll think if they come to me? That is, if I can think at all. What about a blown nervous system? At an extreme that means the famous irreversible coma; but it shades back from there into a grim fog of lost self-awareness and social contact. How do I locate where the shading stops? What if one person in the crowd around my bed holds out for a miracle? Might I, in a body that has stopped communicating, discover at the end that I still want to live? I put down the pencil and turn to easier thoughts.

Then I remember: Drawing these lines isn't for me alone.

So I go to John Luce at San Francisco General Hospital, a place famous for its emergency and trauma teams, AIDS and cancer work, and pediatric clinics. Like every big public hospital, it's full of people in extremis. As an associate director of the medical-surgical intensive-care unit, Luce works on the line every day, standing over blank, silent bodies and considering whether to support life or not—more precisely whether what's there may be so different from the "life" we think we know that the humane act is to let it stop. Luce also thinks and writes about the ethics of what he does.

We talk about people we've seen when he's taken me on rounds in the ICU—most particularly about those who would have been surprised if they'd known they were there.

"Like Carlo here," Luce says as we pause at the swinging doors of the ICU. "I'm sure he never gave it a thought."

If you don't want life-sustaining treatment, speak now while you still can.

Carlo is thirty-four. He left his office downtown at 5:30 on a rainy Wednesday evening, riding as a passenger in a friend's car. Halfway home, the car hit a slick spot and skidded into the rear of a gravel truck. Carlo had just unhitched his shoulder belt to reach for his briefcase in the backseat. His head hit the side post and windshield as metal crumpled around him. Police and paramedics had a hard time extracting him, and he arrived in the emergency room an hour and fifteen minutes after the impact, unconscious.

The pupil of his left eye wouldn't constrict. The "blown" pupil meant something was compressing his brain stem, the control center for breathing, cardiovascular activity, and reflexes, including the eye's response to light. Subdural hematoma, the emergency surgeons figured: a hemorrhage pushing down on the top of the brain. They bored holes in his skull to drain the blood, put in a catheter to provide readings on pressure in his head, and sent him to the ICU.

Carlo's wife, Gloria, left their ten-year-old son and six-year-old daughter with her mother. She bit her lip when she saw her husband inert, with machines sucking and hissing around him.

"It's going to be all right," she said into his ear. No response. "I love you, Carlo," she said. "I'm here with you, darling." Later that night, Carlo's brother, Alex, joined her.

Dr. Luce started his rounds at 8:00 the next morning. Carlo's pupils were now equal size, but they didn't respond to light. A bad sign. He was in a coma.

If Carlo had shown no activity in his brain, he would have been dead by the standards most states have recognized since 1981. But he could breathe on his own and he had some reflexes; the deeper, older parts of his brain still worked. The main damage was in his neocortex ("cortex" means rind or bark), the folded outer layer, the newest part of the brain to evolve. In this layer, less than a quarter of an inch thick, reside a person's senses, control of movement, and awareness.

Luce shouted "Carlo! Carlo!" in his ear, but nothing happened. He pressed a knuckle hard on Carlo's forehead and ground down on his breastbone. The most Carlo did was to go into "extensor posture"—stretching his legs and arms, palms out—a primitive brain-stem reflex that you can see in a laboratory frog when you push on the right place.

Gloria came to the hospital every day; so did Alex. They interpreted Carlo's posture movements as a response to their presence. "See?" Gloria would say. "He's getting better."

The doctors didn't think so. They saw no improvement in ten days; most times that means they'll never see any. One of them disagreed: A young vascular surgeon insisted, "We aren't *certain*. He deserves a chance." Still, he did agree it was time to move Carlo out of intensive care to a step-down unit, a ward where nurses watch for improvements without the ICU's fancy machinery.

In his heart, Alex found himself siding with the doctors; in the face of Gloria's hope, though, he said nothing.

"I think," he told Gloria one day, after a month in the ward, "we should let nature take its course. . . . "

"No," she said.

"We cannot keep him here forever," he said.

She nodded. She couldn't take care of Carlo at home; he needed everything done for him. Besides, she had to work. "I'll take him to a nursing home, I guess," she said. She didn't know how she would pay the tremendous expense of endless care that everyone kept telling her would not lead him back to health.

Then Carlo developed pneumonia. Now somebody had to decide: Withhold treatment and let him die? Give him antibiotics and mechanical ventilation?

Alex said, at last, "No more treatment. Let him go. He wouldn't want this."

"You don't *know* what he'd want," Gloria retorted, shocked. Then, after a long silence, she whispered, "I don't know what he wants. I just want him back." At her request, they started Carlo on antibiotics.

As for the doctors, no matter how strongly they might have believed Carlo would never get better, a family sending mixed messages left them but one choice: Continue all possible treatment.

"The physician's primary ethical stance is beneficence," John Luce said later, "doing what's right for the patient. Of course, that's as the *doctor* decides what's right. The patient might not decide things the same way. So you get to another issue of medical ethics: the patient's autonomy. A patient has a right to refuse therapies, or demand them."

Carlo was about to be wheeled back to the ICU when Gloria resolved the situation. "You really believe he's going to be like this always?" she asked the neurosurgeon.

"One of us is still more hopeful than the others. But my answer is yes."

"Then," she said, "I will take your advice.

I think it will be best for him if you do not give him medicine and do not take him back to intensive care."

There was no plug to be pulled. Carlo's tube-feeding continued. What stopped was the suctioning, medication, and other special care to combat his pneumonia. Three days later, he died.

Once you're unconscious or incompetent, other people will make choices for you. There are two ways to help them.

NOW THAT MEDICAL technology can keep vital fluids and gases pumping almost indefinitely, head trauma is just one of many insults to the body that turn us back to more ancient concerns—as John Luce says, "into the area of what you might call the soul, beyond mere biology." The people around the bed often confront the question, "What does life consist of?"

"That's not a question a doctor should have to answer at the bedside," Luce declares. "It's a question that people should answer for themselves."

Once you're unconscious or incompetent, other people will make choices for you. There are two ways to help them.

The best known is a "living will," a document in which you state the types of treatment you want, and how far you want them to go. This is better than nothing, but it has flaws. You must make the language specific and complete, so you could find yourself writing for twenty pages. If you're brief, a doctor might say, "This is too vague," and disregard it. A living will doesn't take effect until you're terminally ill, and definitions of *terminal* vary widely from state to state, from "imminent death" to "death within several months."

More efficient than a living will is a "durable power of attorney for health care." You appoint someone you trust to make health-care decisions for you if you

can't. It applies in all situations when you can't communicate, not just those in which you're terminally ill. If the person you've appointed wants to withhold or withdraw life-sustaining treatment, the doctor must try to discover if you object; if he or she thinks you do, your treatments continue.

According to the Society for the Right to Die/Concern for Dying, in New York City, forty-one states and the District of Columbia have laws recognizing the validity of living wills. Massachusetts, Michigan, Nebraska, New Jersey, New York, Ohio, Pennsylvania, Rhode Island, and South Dakota do not.

All fifty states and D.C. authorize the general durable power ordinarily used for property and money matters. Eleven make no mention of medical decisions: Alabama, Connecticut, Massachusetts, Michigan, Missouri, Montana, Nebraska, New Hampshire, North Dakota, Oklahoma, and South Carolina. Of the rest, seventeen states and D.C. specifically authorize decisions to withhold or withdraw life support. These states are California, Georgia, Illinois, Kansas, Kentucky, Maine, Mississippi, Nevada, Ohio, Oregon, Rhode Island, South Dakota, Tennessee, Texas, Vermont, West Virginia, and Wisconsin.

A durable power has flaws too. It can't help people who have no one to appoint, and it can tempt you to stick someone else with your responsibilities—without thinking through the particulars.

So make both a living will and a durable power of attorney for health care. They reinforce each other. Make sure your doctor knows about them and includes copies with your medical records. You'll want your durable power to appoint someone who knows you well and whom you trust, and you'll want your family and friends to know what you want.

If you know yourself. I've had forms for a durable power of attorney for health care in my office for three years. I'll think about them today. Or maybe tomorrow.

Reprinted from John Poppy, "End Game," *Esquire*, August 1990, 75–76.

As you have noticed, the article focuses on living wills and durable powers of attorney. Following are the forms for such documents, which are legally accepted in the state of Maryland.

MARYLAND DECLARATION

Declaration made this...day of...... (month, year). I,.......being of sound mind, willfully and voluntarily direct that my dying shall not be artificially prolonged under the circumstances set forth in this declaration.

If at any time I should have an incurable injury, disease, or illness certified to be a terminal condition by two (2) physicians who have personally examined me, one (1) of whom shall be my attending physician, and the physicians have determined that my death is imminent and will occur whether or not life-sustaining procedures are utilized and where the application of such procedures would serve only to artificially prolong the dying process, I direct that such procedures be withheld or withdrawn, and that I be permitted to die naturally with only the administration of medication, the administration of food and water, and the performance of any medical procedure that is necessary to provide comfort care or alleviate pain. In the absence of my ability to give directions regarding the use of such life-sustaining procedures, it is my intention that this declaration shall be honored by my family and physician(s) as the final expression of my right to control my medical care and treatment.

Other instructions: ....
I am legally competent to make this declaration, and I understand its full import. **(Signature and address)**

Under penalty of perjury, we state that this declaration was signed by ....in the presence of the undersigned who, at his/her request, in his/her presence, and in the presence of each other, have hereunto signed our names and witnessed this.....day of.....,19.... Further each of us, individually, states that: The declarant is known to me, and I believe the declarant to be of sound mind. I did not sign the declarant's signature to this declaration. Based upon information and belief, I am not related to the declarant by blood or marriage, a creditor of the declarant, entitled to any portion of the estate of the declarant under any existing testamentary instrument of the declarant, entitled to any financial benefit by reason of the death of the declarant, financially or otherwise responsible for the declarant's medical care, or an employee of any such person or institution. **(Names and addresses of two witnesses)**

MARYLAND DURABLE POWER OF ATTORNEY FOR MEDICAL TREATMENT

This is an important legal document. Before signing this document, it is vital for you to know and understand these facts: This document gives the person you name as your agent the power to make health care decisions for you if you can't make decisions for yourself. Even after you have signed this document, you have the right to make health care decisions for yourself so long as you are able to do so. Your agent will be able to make decisions for you only after two physicians have certified that you are incapable of making them yourself. You have the right to revoke (take away) the authority of your agent by notifying your agent or your health care provider orally or in writing of this desire.

I, **(your name)** hereby appoint: **(agent's name, address and telephone)** as my agent to make health care decisions for me if and when I am unable to make my own health care decisions. This gives my agent the power to consent to giving, withholding or stopping any health care, treatment (including

life-sustaining treatment), service, or diagnostic procedure. I specifically authorize my agent to make decisions for me about artificially supplied nutrition and hydration (tube feeding). My agent also has the authority to talk with health care personnel, get information, and sign forms necessary to carry out those decisions. If the person named as my agent is not available or is unable to act as my agent, then I appoint the following person(s) to serve in the order listed below: 1.**(agent's name, address and telephone)** 2.**(agent's name, address and telephone)**

By this document I intend to create a power of attorney for health care which shall take effect upon my incapacity to make my own health care decisions and shall continue during that incapacity. I have discussed my wishes with my agent, and he or she shall make all health care decisions on my behalf, including decisions to withhold or withdraw all forms of life-sustaining treatment, including artificially administered hydration and nutrition.

My particular wishes are:................
BY SIGNING HERE I INDICATE THAT I UNDERSTAND THE PURPOSE OF THIS DOCUMENT I sign my name to this form on **(date, address and signature)**

WITNESSES I declare that the person who signed or acknowledged this document is personally known to me, that he/she signed or acknowledged this durable power of attorney in my presence, and that he/she appears to be of sound mind and under no duress, fraud, or undue influence. I am not the person appointed as agent by this document, nor am I the patient's health care provider, or an employee of the patient's health care provider. I further declare that I am not related to the patient by blood, marriage, or adoption, and, to the best of my knowledge, I am not entitled to any part of his/her estate under a will now existing or by operation of law. **(Name, address, signature and date of witness 1 and witness 2)**

Discussion Questions

1. What are the legal and medical definitions of death?
2. Is there a difference between ending medical treatment and ending feeding?
3. What is meant by "mercy killing" (euthanasia)?
4. Is it fair to ask someone else to make the decision on whether to continue your life (as in the durable power of attorney)?
5. How does your religion view terminating medical treatment?
6. Under what, if any, conditions do you think human life can be ended?

Practice 1

Prepare a Reading Report on the article. Consider whether you would be willing to sign either or both of these documents, and include your decision with any other comments you wish to make about the article in your Response section of the Reading Report.

Practice 2

This thought-provoking article raises more questions about the ethical problems of terminating treatment than it answers. Divide into small groups, discuss your responses to the article, and formulate a list of the problems associated with this moral dilemma. After the group discussions, each group will report what it considers to be the main ethical issues.

Practice 3

The following sentences contain key words and phrases from the readings. Paraphrase the parts indicated to show that you understand their meaning. Try to do this practice without using a dictionary.

1. "Which '*life-sustaining*' treatments—CPR, mechanical ventilation, surgery, dialysis, drugs?"
2. "Which '*burdens*'—poverty, pain, lost body parts?"
3. " . . . whether what's there may be so different from the 'life' we think we know that *the **humane** act is to let it stop*."
4. "'You don't know what he'd want,' *Gloria **retorted***, shocked."
5. "As for doctors, no matter how strongly they might have believed Carlo would never get better, a family *sending **mixed messages*** left them but one choice: Continue all possible treatment."
6. "Once you're unconscious or **incompetent**, other people will make choices for you."
7. "You must make the language specific and complete, so you could find yourself writing for twenty pages. If you're too brief, a doctor might say, '*This is too **vague***,' and disregard it."
8. "*A durable power has **flaws*** too. It can't help people who have no one to appoint, and it can tempt you to stick someone else with your responsibilities—without thinking through the particulars."

Check Your Progress

Look at the following useful words from the readings. If there are any you don't recognize or know how to use, consider adding them to your vocabulary list.

explicit	ethics	confront
terminated	interpret	consist of
prospect	inert	specific
grim	tremendous	terminally ill
in advance	indefinitely	authorize
hold out for	pull the plug	

Narrowing Your Topic

As you have discovered, this is a very complex issue, and one article cannot give you enough information to make an informed decision or to even discuss it with others without either getting off the subject or resorting to overgeneralizations. Thus, when you are reading about and discussing important and controversial topics, you must focus on a particular part of the problem. If you wish to find more articles on the subject, you will first have to narrow your topic to more specific aspects of the problem, the ones that concern you most. In many instances, you will be able to make decisions about the topic of the articles from the title or from the type of magazine in which it appears.

Look back at the sample page from the *Readers' Guide*. If, for example, you wish to find out more about how Christianity views the problem, you will be able to make an informed guess that the entry "Has the 'right to die' arrived?" in *Christianity Today* cites an article that discusses this aspect of the topic. If you wish to read about the legal aspect, any one of the articles which discuss the Supreme Court decision on the Cruzan case will provide such information. It is not always possible to find an article about the specific aspect of the subject you want by title and magazine, and there will be times when you will have to find and skim through several articles before you find the exact information you want. However, using this method is generally a satisfactory and more efficient way of finding articles about a subject than simply looking through magazines and newspapers randomly.

Practice 4

Choose one of the ethical problems your group identified in Practice 2. Go to the library and, using an index, find an article on the problem your group has chosen to explore. Look back at the *Readers' Guide* sample page for ideas on subject headings you could use. After you have located possible articles in the index, check the serials list to see if the library has the issue of the magazine you need. Then, find the article. Each member of the group should prepare a Reading Report on it and come to class prepared to have an in-depth discussion of that issue.

Practice 5

With your group, decide on one of the topics for further investigation and, if possible, go to the library together. Look in the subject entries to find books on the subject you have selected. Each person in the group should find a different book on the same topic. Locate the books and check them out. Bring the books to the next class meeting.

Topics for Further Investigation

1. Genetic engineering
2. Euthanasia
3. "Test tube" babies
4. Surrogate mothers
5. Experimentation on animals
6. Use of experimental drugs on humans

Which do you prefer to read, fact or fiction? Bestsellers such as *The Accidental Tourist* and *You Just Don't Understand: Women and Men in Conversation* can be found in the library.

How to Write a Book Report

Reporting on Fiction and Nonfiction

One of the activities you will be doing in this course is reading a book and writing a book report, and perhaps making an oral report to the class. This may be the first time you have read an entire book in English. It is therefore especially important that you choose one that you will enjoy reading. Books are generally classified as "fiction" or "nonfiction." Fiction refers to novels or stories that the author has created or imagined. Works of fiction are not true, while nonfiction books are factual and are supposed to be true. Biographies and autobiographies are works of nonfiction, and there are books on every subject you can imagine, from automobiles to zoos.

You may select either a fiction or nonfiction book to read. You may want to read a spy thriller, a detective story, a romance novel, a best seller, or a book that has been made into a movie, or you may choose to read about a famous person or some other nonfiction topic that interests you. When selecting your book, try reading a few pages to see if the work captures your attention. If it doesn't, try another one. It is not necessary to understand every word, but you should be able to follow the general idea of the book.

After you have finished reading, you will write a book report, which is similar to a Reading Report. You may also be asked to make an oral report to the class. Your written report will only be about 500 or 600 words long, and it will not be as formal as a book review. A book review of a work of fiction, for example, analyzes characters, discusses themes, and critiques the literary style of the author.

For our purposes, however, if you are reading fiction, your report will include a summary of the plot, what you found interesting/ unusual/good/bad about the book, and your opinion of it. You should also tell who the main characters are and mention where the story takes place. If you are reporting on a nonfiction book, identify the purpose of the book, tell something about the author, and then mention some of the ideas you found particularly interesting.

In this lesson, we are going to look at reports on a work of fiction, *The Accidental Tourist* by the American author Anne Tyler, and a nonfiction work entitled *You Just Don't Understand: Women and Men in Conversation*, by a sociolinguist named Deborah Tannen.

The Accidental Tourist has been made into a very popular movie that is available on videotape. We hope that you will have an oppor- tunity to see the movie before you read the book report. Then you will have a good understanding of the characters and the plot, and you will see how this quantity of information is written in a report. For *You Just Don't Understand*, we have prepared a fairly lengthy summary for you to read and discuss so that you will understand what the book is about before you read the book report.

Practice 1

If you are able to watch the movie, *The Accidental Tourist*, complete the following worksheet as you watch.

Worksheet for *The Accidental Tourist*

Major characters:

Minor characters:

Location:

What happened in the story:

List two or three interesting, unusual, or amusing things that happened:

Why you liked or didn't like the movie:

Practice 2

In small groups, share your worksheets and discuss your opinion of the movie. What do you think the theme of this story is?

Book Report for *The Accidental Tourist*

Title: *The Accidental Tourist*

Author: Anne Tyler

Publisher: Alfred A. Knopf, Inc.

Date: 1985

Summary:

This is the funny yet sad story of Macon Leary, a writer of guide books for business travelers who hate to leave home, and his relationships with his eccentric brothers and sister, his estranged wife, and a wacky young woman, Muriel Pritchett. Macon's previously orderly life is disrupted when his wife Sarah leaves him a year after the senseless killing of their 12-year-old son, Ethan, in a fast food restaurant where he had gone for a hamburger. Macon is living like a hermit in their home with only Helen, the cat, and Edward, the unruly but loveable dog, as companions. When Macon breaks his leg, he and Edward move back to the family homestead to be cared for by his two divorced brothers who live there with their unmarried sister.

The Leary household, where everyone loves order and perhaps even more the creating of order, has difficulty adjusting to Edward, who attacks the rare visitors to the Leary home, refuses to obey, and seems to be untrainable. It is then that the dog trainer Muriel, the divorced mother of a young son, enters the story. Muriel, whose life and friends are filled with chaos and fun, is the direct opposite of Macon and his family. She challenges the well-ordered Leary existence, helps Macon to overcome the grief of his son's death, and brings him back into direct involvement with others and with life, which he had previously approached almost as an observer. Once Macon learns to accept Muriel's undisciplined but fun-filled way of life, he is forced to choose between it or a retreat to the safety of what he had always known.

Response:

I saw the movie version of this book a couple of years ago, and that is why I decided to read it. I'm certainly glad I did. The book is really enjoyable. It's funny—the Learys are an unbelievable family!—and at the same time, it's sad. Anne Tyler's writing is clear, direct, and vivid. The novel takes place in Baltimore, and Tyler makes you feel as if you're really there. Her people talk and behave the way real people do, not always saying or doing what they would actually like.

There are two things in the book that really struck me. One is the Leary family itself. How unusual it is to find an American family of adult brothers and sister living happily together in the old family home! But then, who else could put up with their overly organized way of life. They even put their groceries away in the cupboard in alphabetical order. And do you know anyone who could ignore a ringing telephone (for weeks at a time) simply because he or she doesn't want to talk to one person? The whole Leary family does. But at the same time, they are charming and all have the wonderful fault of having no sense of direction. They seldom leave the house because even a trip to the local hardware store, their favorite place to visit, means taking the chance that they won't be able to find their way home.

Another amusing aspect of the book is Macon's approach to travel—that it is always better to stay home, but if one must travel, one should be protected from disruptive, foreign influences and try to remain psychologically at home. He turns this attitude into the basis for his work, the writing of travel guide books for others who are "accidental tourists." While it is true that many business travelers probably grow tired of being away and search for ways to make themselves feel "at home" when they are, I find it hard to believe that very many Americans traveling to Paris would search out restaurants which serve "tasty American food."

All in all, this is a wonderful book. Read it and enjoy!

Read and discuss the following summary before reading the book report on it.

Summary of *You Just Don't Understand: Women and Men in Conversation*

Why can't men and women understand each other? Who talks more, men or women? Is there a difference in the way men talk to other men and the way women talk to other women? What do men and women each want from their conversations? Deborah Tannen, a professor of linguistics at Georgetown University, provides some startling answers to these and other fascinating questions in her best-selling book, *You Just Don't Understand: Women and Men in Conversation*, published by William Morrow and Company in 1990.

The author of many academic books and scholarly articles, Deborah Tannen has succeeded in bringing her sociolinguistic research to the general public, and the public has loved it. The book was on the *New York Times* Best-Seller List for more than a year, and Tannen became an overnight celebrity, appearing as a guest on all the major TV network talk shows. Clearly, people want to know more about how men and women communicate.

Tannen analyzed numerous recordings and videotapes of everyday conversations of children, teenagers, and adults to study how people interact and how they use conversation to satisfy their needs. Her research led her to the conclusion that American "boys and girls grow up in what are essentially different cultures, so talk between women and men is cross-cultural communication." This may seem like a radical approach—to claim that we need to examine the conversational styles of American men and women as communication between people of two different cultures.

Certainly, Tannen makes a strong and convincing case for using a cross-cultural approach for understanding the communication and *mis*communication between men and women of the United States. Citing her research and that of other sociolinguists, anthropologists, and psychologists, she states:

Even if they grow up in the same neighborhood, on the same block, or in the same house, girls and boys grow up in different worlds of words. Others talk to them differently and expect and accept different ways of talking from them. Most important, children learn how to talk, how to have conversations, not only from their parents but from their peers.

Researchers have documented that boys and girls spend most of their time playing with other children of the same sex and that the way that boys and girls talk to their friends is very different. Boys tend to play outside and prefer games involving large groups which have leaders and systems of rules to determine the winners and the losers. In their play, boys are primarily concerned about establishing and maintaining their status in the hierarchy of the group. Status is achieved by giving orders and getting others to follow them, or by telling jokes or stories to keep the other boys' attention focused on them. Boys spend their playtime *doing*. Their talk is centered on giving commands, boasting about what they can do, or arguing about who can do something best.

The world of little girls presents a stark contrast. Girls tend to play indoors in small groups or with just one other girl, especially their best friend. They spend much of their time sitting and talking, sharing secrets to maintain their closeness. Girls play games where they take turns, and winning or losing is not very important. Indeed, in many of the activities that girls prefer, such as playing house, there are no winners or losers. Girls are more likely to be concerned about how everyone is getting along together. Instead of giving orders, they tend to make suggestions such as "Let's do this" or "Why don't you do this and I'll do that." Their status is measured by how well they are liked by other girls in their group. Whereas "independence and freedom" are important to boys, "intimacy and connection" are the goals of girls' conversations.

The attitudes and conversational priorities we see in children's play, Tannen says, carry over into the lives of adult men and women and how they view life and the role of conversation in their relationships. For men, life is "a contest, a struggle to preserve independence and avoid failure." They are constantly assessing their positions in the social hierarchy where they are always either "one-up" or "one-down." Tannen asserts, "In this world [a man's world], conversations are negotiations in which people try to achieve and maintain the upper hand if they can, and protect themselves from others' attempts to put them down and push them around."

For women, on the other hand, life is "a community, a struggle to preserve intimacy and avoid isolation." Women see people as individuals in a "network of connections." Tannen writes, "In this world [a woman's world], conversations are negotiations for closeness in which people try to seek and give confirmation and support, and to reach consensus. They try to protect themselves from others' attempts to push them away."

In studying videotapes of girls and boys and men and women talking to their best friends (of the same sex), Tannen was struck by the fact that there were remarkable similarities in the conversations of the girls and women of all ages. The conversations of the boys and men of different ages were very similar as well.

The differences showed up when comparisons were made between the boys and girls of the same age. Indeed, they were so different in both the content of the conversation and the body language of the speakers that Tannen said the females and males sometimes looked like they had come from different planets. The girls and women sat close together, faced each other directly, and looked into each others' eyes when they talked. They took turns talking about each others' problems and about other people they knew, and made supportive statements that said, "I know what you mean. That is my experience, too. We are the same."

The boys and men, on the other hand, did not sit as close together, tended to have more open body positions, sat at angles to each other, and had very little eye contact. They showed their caring for each other by teasing and joking. For men and boys, offering sympathy puts the other in a "one-down" position, so when they talked about their problems, they reassured each other by offering quick advice, and telling the other that it really wasn't a problem and he really shouldn't worry about it. Or, they changed the subject.

Although these patterns seem to work well when people talk to someone of the same sex, they can be the source of misunderstanding and even pain when women and men try to talk to each other. When a woman tells a man about a problem, she expects sympathy and expressions of support. If the man responds by offering quick advice instead, or by trying to convince her that it is really not a serious problem, she will probably feel that he doesn't care about her. Boys and men raise an issue, come up with a solution, and then go on to another topic. Women want to discuss an issue at length, ask questions, give and receive support and sympathy, and if there is a disagreement, women want to reach a solution that everyone can agree on.

Tannen offers numerous examples of miscommunications between couples. A wife was anxious to return home to her family after being in the hospital. She complained about how painful it was to get around in the house, and her husband responded that perhaps she should have stayed in the hospital longer. His giving her advice instead of sympathy made her feel like he didn't want her around.

Men frequently focus on the words being spoken, unaware that another message about the relationship is being communicated at the same time. A good example of this is a conversation which takes place in the novel *The Accidental Tourist* by Anne Tyler. Although Macon, the man, is still married to someone else, he has been living with his girlfriend, Muriel. One evening he comments that he doesn't think that Muriel's son, Alexander, is getting a good education:

"I asked him to figure what change they'd give back when we bought the milk today, and he didn't have the faintest idea. He didn't even know he'd have to subtract."

"Well, he's only in second grade," Muriel said.

"I think he ought to switch to a private school."

"Private schools cost money."

"So? I'll pay."

She stopped flipping the bacon and looked over at him. "What are you saying, Macon? Are you saying that you're committed?"

Muriel goes on to tell Macon that he must make up his mind whether he wants to divorce his wife and marry her: She can't put her son in a new school and then have to pull him out when and if Macon returns to his wife. The conversation ends with Macon saying, incredulously, "But I just want him to learn to subtract!"

While Macon is thinking only of the simple question of how Alexander can best learn to subtract, Muriel hears another, potentially very important message: his willingness to pay for her son's attending a private school could signal a significant change in their relationship.

It is ironic that home, the place where one should be able to feel completely relaxed and understood, may be the scene of some of the worst misunderstandings between men and women. Husbands and wives interpret what each other says from their own perspective, not realizing that they are engaging in cross-cultural communication.

One of the reasons for these misunderstandings, according to Tannen, may be how women view public and private speech. Many men are more comfortable with public speech where they defend their positions and exchange information. In public situations, men speak more than women. When they come home, however, men want to relax and read the newspaper. "Men are afraid of being left out by not knowing what is going on in the world," Dr. Tannen reports. Men are much more interested in knowing about the news than they are in discussing what is happening to other people.

This is very frustrating to their wives, who are eager to talk about the details of other people's lives—their friends, family members, and business associates. For women, the purpose of conversation is interaction. Keeping up to date about friends and others is a pleasure; indeed, it may be an obligation for women. Most women talk on the phone to their best friend at least once a week. They are frustrated because their husbands do not want to talk to them in the same way that their women friends do. Women often complain that their husbands never tell them enough details.

Men wonder what their wives are complaining about. They may go for long periods of time without talking to their men friends about their personal lives. For men, the purpose of conversation is to impart information. They do not like small talk; it does not communicate information. Men generally spend much shorter amounts of time on the telephone, for example. Students living away at college report that when they call home, most of the phone conversation is with their mother. Their father may come on the phone briefly to discuss some specific issue, but he does not chat at length like his wife does.

The fact that women are more comfortable with private talk than they are with public talk puts them at a disadvantage in the public arena. Women are not accustomed to fighting for a chance to speak during a meeting, for example. Because women are used to waiting for their turn to speak, they are frequently ignored by men who expect that if they have something to say, they will speak up, as a man would do. Because women are generally good listeners, asking questions and making supportive comments, they may find that men are lecturing them, instead of asking them what *they* think, as another woman would do.

This may help explain why there are so few women who hold public office, Tannen suggests. In order to run for office, a woman has to be able to campaign like a man and employ many of the conversation strategies used by men. In so doing, however, she appears to be *unwomanly*, and may therefore not be trusted. Tannen cites the case of Geraldine Ferraro, who ran for Vice President of the United States, and was criticized for being too aggressive and pushy.

Tannen concludes that it is important to understand the differences in the conversational styles of men and women so that we can better interpret the messages that are being communicated. Men and women have something to learn from each other. Neither style is right or wrong; they are just different. Once we understand that women and men "often have different assumptions about the world and about ways of talking, people are very creative about figuring out how this rift is affecting their own relationships." Although we might not be able to prevent disagreements, we may at least keep them from getting out of control. Understanding each others' styles of speaking as women and men is the first step to understanding each other as individuals.

Questions for Discussion

1. How does the way that girls play and the way that boys play create different "cultures" for them to grow up in? What do they do? How do they each achieve status in their respective groups? Was this your experience as a child?

2. How does Tannen say that men and women each view life? How does each therefore view the role of conversation in relationships? Do you think that women and men are like that?

3. What body language did Tannen observe in the videotaped conversations of girls and women and boys and men talking to their best friends? When you talk to your best friend (of the same sex), how do you show you care for each other?

4. When a man tells another man about a problem, what happens? What does a woman expect when she tells another woman about a problem? What happens when a man and a woman discuss a problem? Have you ever seen "cross-cultural miscommunication" occur under these circumstances?

5. What was the source of misunderstanding in the scene from *The Accidental Tourist*? Has this ever happened to you? How would you interpret the conversation, as Macon did, or as Muriel did?

6. What is the difference in the way women and men handle public and private speech? How does this result in misunderstandings?

7. Why are there so few women in public office? What do you think of women political leaders? What kind of speaking style do they have? Do women leaders appear pushy or aggressive?

8. Who really talks more, men or women?

9. Are the observations that Tannen makes about American women and men true for women and men in your country? Are there any differences? Could the term "cross-cultural communication" apply for the opposite sexes in your country?

Book Report for *You Just Don't Understand*

Title: *You Just Don't Understand: Women and Men in Conversation*

Author: Deborah Tannen

Publisher: William Morrow and Company

Date: 1990

Summary:

If you have ever wondered why there are so many misunderstandings between men and women, you will want to read Deborah Tannen's book, *You Just Don't Understand*. Tannen, a professor of sociolinguistics at Georgetown University, says that the source of the problem is that men and women are really engaging in cross-cultural communication. The experiences they have growing up are so different that they are really raised in different cultures.

After viewing videotapes of girls and boys talking to their best friends, for example, Tannen concluded that the girls and boys sometimes acted as if they came from different planets. The girls shared secrets, sat close together, looked into each other's eyes, took turns talking about their problems, and made sympathetic comments to each other. The boys, on the other hand, teased and joked with each other, and when discussing problems tended to offer quick advice, minimized the importance of the problem, or even changed the subject.

These conversational patterns, Tannen says, carry over into adulthood and may cause serious misunderstandings between the sexes. Men are very concerned about their place in the hierarchy of the social group, and therefore see conversations as "negotiations in which people try to achieve and maintain the upper hand if they can, and protect themselves from others' attempts to put them down and push them around."

Women, in contrast, are concerned with building and maintaining intimate relationships. They view conversations as "negotiations for closeness in which people try to seek and give confirmation and support, and to reach consensus. They try to protect themselves from others' attempts to push them away."

Not being aware of these differences, women may be surprised and frustrated when they tell their husband about a problem and, rather than discussing it at length and offering sympathy (as another woman would do), the man offers a quick piece of advice. By the same token, men cannot understand why women want to spend so much time going over and over a problem.

Response:

I was really impressed with this book. In the first place, I am very interested in the research that Tannen has done and in the whole question of how people use language to satisfy their needs. But on the personal level, I found it particularly enlightening because it gave me insight into how men and women approach conversation. After reading the book, I understood why men don't like to talk on the phone, for example. Tannen says that most men do not like small talk, and they try to get off the phone as quickly as possible. Many women, on the other hand, spend large amounts of time on the phone maintaining close relationships with their friends. There are long conversations about who said what to whom, and how everyone is getting along.

Tannen makes the point that neither conversational style is "right" or "wrong"—they are just different. Men and women have something to learn from each other, as do any two people who come from different cultures. Perhaps if more people read Tannen's book, they would know what to expect from the opposite sex, and there wouldn't be so many misunderstandings. I would certainly recommend that you read it. It might even save your marriage someday!

Tips for Writing a Book Report

1. State the title (underlined), author, publisher, and date of publication, and make a general statement of what the book is about in the first sentence. (See longer summary of *You Just Don't Understand*.) Or, you may list the publication information (as is done for the two book reports in this lesson) at the beginning of your report.

   Example of an opening paragraph for fiction:

   One Fine Day the Rabbi Bought a Cross, written by Harry Kemelman and published by Ballantine Books in 1987, is the latest in a series of mystery stories about the adventures of Rabbi Small.

   Example of an opening paragraph for nonfiction:

   Anthony Robbins, the master of mind power, has written a guide to personal achievement—*Unlimited Power*, published by Random House in 1989.

2. If you are writing a book report on fiction, make a summary of the book and include these points:
   - The setting: time, location
   - The characters
   - A summary of the plot
   - The theme or central idea
   - Your opinion of the book and why
   - Comments about any aspect of the story (unusual, interesting, funny, sad)

3. If you are writing a book report on nonfiction, make a summary and include these points:
   - Information about the author
   - The purpose of the book
   - A summary of the important points
   - An example of particular interest to you
   - Your opinion of the book and why
   - Comments about any aspect of it

Practice 3

Write a book report following the instructions in this lesson.

Activities to Help You Improve Your Coursework

Have you heard about "World Music"? Read about musicians such as Paul Simon and Ladysmith Black Mambazo in "Sing, and the whole world sings with you—now in any language" on pages 53 and 54.

Acquiring New Vocabulary

In this course, it is important to read for information and main ideas and not worry about understanding every word. Much vocabulary can be understood and even learned by guessing at meanings by using context clues, and noticing how the word is used when it appears again. If you have a good overview of what the article is about, you will find that it is much easier to guess the meaning of unfamiliar words.

Reading Without Using Your Dictionary

The reading selection for this chapter, "Sing, and the Whole World Sings with You—Now in Any Language," is about music. The subtitle, "So-called world music exposing Westerners to non-English acts; 'Graceland' led way," tells us that Westerners are now hearing musical groups from all over the world, singing in languages other than English.

Do you know what "Graceland" is? If you do, you already have a good overview of what this article is about. If you do not, before you read the article look for information about "Graceland." You will find it under the subheading "Graceland." What is it? In this section of the article, the author tells us that "Graceland" was a "milestone" in the world music movement. What do you think a "milestone" is? Use context clues to guess the meaning. Remember that the subtitle tells us that Graceland "led (the) way." What do you think the main idea of this article is?

Practice 1

The first paragraph may contain unfamiliar words and it may therefore appear to be difficult. Instead of worrying about the words that you do *not* know, focus on those you *do* know. Use a highlighter to color all the words you know. Read the paragraph and then answer these questions:

1. Are the ten men wearing western clothing? Where are they from? Are they singing or dancing?
2. What country are the twenty-six women from? How are they dressed? What are they doing?
3. What instrument is the person from Brazil playing? Is he dressed in his native clothing? What language is he singing in?

If you are able to answer these questions, you have understood the basic idea of the paragraph: Two groups of singers and a guitarist are singing songs in their native languages, dressed in their native clothing. These people are identified in the third paragraph. The African group is called Ladysmith Black Mambazo. What is the Bulgarian group called? What is the name of the Brazilian guitarist?

From this exercise you should see that focusing on the words and phrases you *know* will allow you to understand the basic idea, even if you cannot get all the details. You may wish to use this technique of highlighting all the words you know in other readings in order to help you figure out main ideas in articles which seem particularly difficult at first glance.

SPECIALIZED VOCABULARY

1. a cappella—singing without any accompaniment on a musical instrument

2. harmony—the chords that are played along with the melody

3. folk music—the traditional songs of a people

4. flamenco—a type of music from Spain

5. act—a performer or musical group performing at a concert

6. tour—a trip where an artist gives many concerts in different cities

7. emcee—a word created from saying the letters "M.C.," which stand for "Master of Ceremonies"; an emcee introduces the performers at a concert or the speakers at a meeting

8. talent agent—a person who looks for musicians to record for a record company

9. venue—the place where a concert takes place

10. reggae—a type of music from the Caribbean

11. label—a piece of paper telling the contents of something; here it refers to the paper on a record which tells the name of the recording company, or it refers to the recording company itself

12. a hit—a very popular song that sells many records

13. pop chart—the list of the most popular songs, published every week

14. lyrics—the words to a song

Sing, and the whole world sings with you—now in any language

So-called world music exposing Westerners to non-English acts; 'Graceland' led way

By KEVIN ZIMMERMAN

New York Ten men in African tribal dress lift their voices in a cappella harmony. Twenty-six women in traditional Bulgarian garb sing out in their native tongue. A Brazilian guitarist arrayed in flamboyant attire sings passionately in Portuguese.

These are not uncommon performances in the singers' own countries, and they are becoming more common in the U.S.

Ladysmith Black Mambazo, Le Mystère des Voix Bulgares and Milton Nascimento are part of what has been dubbed world music, and they are helping to build U.S. interest for that music. World music already has found a place on British, German and Japanese charts.

Native tongue

The world music label loosely refers to any non-English-speaking musician singing in his native tongue. As with Ladysmith and Le Mystère, the genre sometimes is blurred with folk music, but the natural rhythms of their singing and the beat heard in the music of King Sunny Adé or "new flamenco" artists Pata Negra and Gipsy Kings appeals to those brought up on rock 'n' roll.

Members of the rock community have been experimenting with pan-world rhythms for some time. Talking Heads often has used African and Caribbean styles in its music; Peter Gabriel, who penned a stirring tribute to South African martyr Steven Biko, explores African themes in his music and featured Senegal's Youssou N'Dour as opening act on his 1986 tour.

'Graceland'

But it was Paul Simon, with his 1986 "Graceland" album and tour, who blew the scene wide open for U.S. audiences. The album features Simon and a South African band performing in the mbaqanga style, marked by its distinctive beat. On tour, Simon served more as emcee than headlining artist, introducing Ladysmith, Hugh Masekela and Miriam Makeba and exposing Western audiences to decidedly non-Western music.

"Paul Simon introduced African culture to American audiences who had no idea what was going on before," says Brad Gelfond, senior talent agent at Triad Artists who booked the "Graceland" tour.

Robert Browning, director of the World Music Institute, which produces numerous world music concerts in New York, also hails "Graceland" as "definitely a milestone."

Many people who saw the "Graceland" concerts agree that Ladysmith stole the show, and the group used that experience as a springboard to success. The first album under the band's U.S. deal with Warner Bros., the Simon-produced "Shaka Zulu," won the 1987 Grammy for best traditional folk recording. Its song "Beautiful Rain" accompanies a 7-Up commercial and the group sings at the end of Michael Jackson's "Moonwalker" video.

Perhaps most important, Ladysmith now can tour without record company support or corporate sponsorship. The group has been selling out 3,000-seat venues, according to band spokesman Alberta Rhodes.

Without radio support, touring is the best way for most world music acts to be heard by U.S. audiences. But it's expensive.

"You're usually transporting a minimum of 10 people across international waters, at least 4,000 miles," says Larry Gold, prexy of Third World Agency, which books world music tours throughout North America. "And . . . the production costs are not cheap."

Third World also operates as North American agent for many of the world music artists touring the U.S.

Gold says a relatively well-known African group might draw 3,000 people in a major city, but only 100 elsewhere. "A lot of artists who are superstars in their own country are willing to come down to a lower level here, to break through, to work at a short-term loss for a longterm gain," he says.

"Rhythm Safari," a 40- to 50-city jaunt featuring 3-4 African bands, is scheduled to begin in July. Gelfond hopes to play indoor theaters and outdoor amphitheaters.

He says the time is right for an all-African tour in the wake of the "Graceland" tour and Amnesty Intl.'s "Human Rights Now!"

"People who are in their 20s and 30s have been listening to rock 'n' roll for a long time," says Danny Kahn, director of promotion at Nonesuch. He was instrumental in the label's recent Le Mystère des Voix Bulgares tour. "It's only natural that people try to discover new styles."

(*continued*)

Kahn notes the 3-week tour sold out all its dates except Toronto, playing 3,500-seat venues and attracting about 20,000 people. He says the interest in world music may be just a fad, but is optimistic about continued success for the choir.

Browning also is cautious about the possibility of the music being a passing interest. "That happened with Indian music and Ravi Shankar in particular in the '60s. It grew to where you could sell out the Felt Forum, but it passed."

Gold is bullish on world music, however. He dismisses comparisons to reggae, for which international interest was stunted with the death of Bob Marley in 1981. "I don't see a spearhead of any single group in world music. America can't deal with it on an individual basis. That's why you have terms like 'world beat' or 'ethno-pop.'"

He cites the record industry's interest. What once was the exclusive domain of independent labels like Carthage and Shanachie is becoming more of a major-label proposition. Nonesuch has Le Mystère; Warner Bros. has Ladysmith, Yemenite thrush Ofra Haza and David Byrne's compilation "Brazil Classics I: Beleza Tropical," and Virgin has N'Dour and the "Earthworks" compilations.

"The next step is for an American to have a big hit doing a Brazilian or African influenced song or a Brazilian doing a song that's so rhythmically happening it'll cross over to the pop charts," Gold says. "Once that hit happens, the language barrier will come down. People will get into the music itself rather than the lyrics. Singing in English will not be required any more."

Kevin Zimmerman, "Sing, and the whole world sings with you—now in any language," *Variety*, 22 March 1989, 101–102.

Questions for Discussion

1. What American music stars are popular in your country? What artists from your country are internationally famous?
2. What evidence of the "world music" movement do you see?
3. What kind of music do you like? Who are your favorite recording stars?
4. Have you ever been to a live concert performance of a superstar? Where was it and who sang? How did the audience react?
5. What effect does the American entertainment industry have on the movies and music produced in your country?
6. What do you think the role of the English language should be in the world?

Practice 2

In small groups, discuss the reading and answer the questions above. Then, check your comprehension of the main ideas by answering the questions that follow. Next as a group write up a Reading Report summary, but write your own individual response to the reading. Be sure to begin your summary with a statement of the main idea of the article. When you have finished your reports, exchange summaries with other groups and compare what you have written. Are there any significant differences?

1. What is "world music"?
2. In what countries is it popular?
3. What kind of musicians play it?
4. Who really introduced Americans to world music?
5. What is the significance of "Graceland"? What country are the musicians in the Ladysmith group from?
6. What are two ways that groups from other countries become popular in the United States?
7. What do people in the music industry believe is the future of world music in the United States?

If you were able to answer the questions above, you have understood the main points of the article. This means that you were able to understand the most important information in the article without looking up any words in the dictionary.

Creating Your Own Vocabulary List

As you read an article in English, you use several strategies for dealing with unfamiliar words: you ignore them, try to guess what they mean from the context, or look them up in the dictionary. But how do you decide which words you should look up?

Key Words: Most articles that you read will have certain key vocabulary words that you need to know in order to understand the reading. Sometimes these words are specialized, such as the terms dealing with music used in this reading. In Part A, Lesson 3, the article on the right to die contained specialized vocabulary such as life-sustaining, dialysis, paramedic, tube feeding, and trauma team. Many articles written about terminating treatment will contain these words, so they become *key words* for understanding and discussing the topic of continuing medical treatment when someone is terminally ill.

In addition to these specialized words, there are other key words in the article which are used repeatedly, making them important for understanding it, but these words are less specialized. They have a broader meaning or can be used in a broader variety of contexts. These key words are: humane, flaw, ethics, explicit, confront, authorize.

When reading an article, then, it will be necessary for you to understand the *key words* in that article, whether they are specialized for that particular topic, or have a broader, more general meaning and usefulness. You should first make an attempt to guess the meaning of key words, but if you cannot figure them out, look them up and make note of the definition.

Active and Passive Vocabulary: In this course, you will create your own vocabulary list and decide which words you want to learn. The words you choose are words that you want to be able to use in speaking and writing. They will be part of your *active* vocabulary. You will also be developing your *passive* vocabulary. That is, there will be an even greater number of words that you will learn to *recognize* when you see them in a reading, but you may not know exactly what they mean or be able to use them actively when you speak or write.

As you read, you will be adding to your passive vocabulary constantly, with very little effort. To increase your active vocabulary, however, you will have to make an effort to use the word as you learn it, in order to make it yours. Words that you decide to add to your active vocabulary should be looked up in the dictionary.

Selecting your vocabulary words: There will be certain vocabulary words in each reading that you will find particularly interesting. You will want to choose several of them to add to your *active* vocabulary. These words may or may not be key words in the reading. You may be drawn to a particular word for a variety of reasons. The most important reason for choosing a word for your vocabulary list is that you believe this word will be useful for you. It is a word you want to be yours.

Remember that for this course you should be following several steps in creating your vocabulary list:

1. Copy the sentence from the reading containing the vocabulary word. This is to show the context in which the word was used.
2. Look up the word in the dictionary and write down what part of speech it is. Is it a noun, verb, adjective, or adverb?
3. Write the definition of the word. If there is more than one definition, choose the one that makes sense for the context of your reading.
4. Use the word in your own original sentence to demonstrate that you understand its meaning and know how to use it.

Here is an example of what you should write for each of your vocabulary words:

"But it was Paul Simon, with his 1986 'Graceland' *album* and tour, who blew the scene wide open for U.S. audiences."

album—noun; a long-playing record or set of records

Record *albums* are no longer as popular as cassette tapes or compact discs; you see very few albums for sale in music stores.

In the example above, there was more than one definition given in the dictionary for the word "album."

al-bum (al′bəm). n. 1. a book consisting of blank leaves, pockets, envelopes, etc., for keeping photographs, stamps, or the like. 2. a long-playing phonograph record or set of records. 3. the container for such a record or records. 4. a visitors' register. [<L: neut. sing. of *albus* white]

Obviously, given the context, definition number two makes the best sense.

It is a good idea to also list other parts of speech with your word. This will help enlarge your vocabulary. "Album" does not have any other forms, but other words in this reading do:

NOUN	VERB	ADJECTIVE	ADVERB
music, musician	—	musical	musically
rhythm	—	rhythmic	rhythmically
performance	perform	performing	—
distinction	—	distinctive	distinctively
decision	decide	decided, decisive	decidedly

When you prepare your vocabulary list, depending on your teacher's instructions, you may write your words on the Reading Report Form, keep a vocabulary notebook, or make vocabulary cards. A goal is to choose three or four words for each reading that you do, but you may find that some readings have more interesting vocabulary than others. What is important is that you select words that you will use so that your active vocabulary will grow steadily. You are more likely to remember and use vocabulary words that you have chosen yourself than those on a list given to you to learn. Once you have added a word to your list, be sure to make a conscious effort to use the word several times over the next few days, and you should review your list every one or two weeks.

Practice 3

The following sentences contain key words and phrases from the reading. Paraphrase the parts indicated to show that you understand their meaning. Try to do this practice without using a dictionary.

1. "A Brazilian guitarist arrayed in flamboyant **attire** sings passionately in Portuguese."
2. "Ladysmith Black Mambazo, Le Mystère des Voix Bulgares and Milton Nascimento are part of *what has been **dubbed** world music*, and they are helping to build U.S. interest for that music."
3. "On tour, Simon served more as emcee than headlining artist, introducing Ladysmith, Hugh Masekela and Miriam Makeba and ***exposing** Western audiences to decidedly non-Western music*."
4. "'Paul Simon introduced African culture to American audiences who had no idea what was going on before,' says Brad Gelfond, senior talent agent at Triad Artists, who ***booked** the 'Graceland' tour*."
5. "Many people who saw the 'Graceland' concerts agree that Ladysmith stole the show, and the group used that experience as a ***springboard** to success*."
6. "'You're usually ***transporting** a minimum of 10 people across international waters, at least 4,000 miles,' says Larry Gold, prexy of Third World Agency, which books world music tours throughout North America."
7. "'A lot of artists who are superstars in their own country are willing to come down to a lower level here, to break through, to work at a ***short-term** loss for a **longterm** gain*,' he says."
8. "Gelfond hopes to play indoor theaters and *outdoor **amphitheaters***."
9. "He says the interest in world music may be *just a **fad***, but is optimistic about continued success for the choir. Browning also is cautious about the possibility of the music being a passing interest."

Check Your Progress

Look at the following useful words from the reading. If there are any you don't recognize or know how to use, consider selecting them to add to your vocabulary list.

perform	optimistic	tribute
theme	domain	distinctive
common, uncommon	independent	exclusive
expose	genre	

Practice 4

Read the following paragraphs and highlight the words you *know*. Practice figuring out the main idea of the reading and guessing the meanings of the unfamiliar words. Decide which words you would ignore, which ones you would spend time trying to figure out the meanings of, and which ones you would want to look up in the dictionary and add to your active vocabulary.

Flying down to Rio

A pop veteran finds the Brazilian beat

Most singer-songwriters write their songs first and then assemble musicians to help turn them into records. Paul Simon does it the other way around. His new album, *The Rhythm of the Saints*, began with a journey to Brazil two years ago. Without any songs in mind, Simon recorded local drummers playing traditional rhythms. Later, he listened to the tapes back home in New York City, improvising melodies and lyrics until songs gradually emerged. With *The Rhythm of the Saints*, hot tropical roots meet the cool breeze of a cerebral pop sensibility.

The record is a logical yet adventurous sequel to *Graceland* (1986), which won the Grammy for album of the year, sold more than four million copies and helped usher black South Africa's voice into the mainstream. Simon sculpted *Graceland's* music around the savannah-soft harmonies of the South African vocal group Ladysmith Black Mambazo. His new record is based on the rich drum culture of Brazil, a legacy handed down from West African slaves. The result is an album that sounds even more insistently African than *Graceland*. Simon's voice floats above dense thickets of percussion, rhythms as tough and sweet as sugarcane. The lyrics once again feature Simon's urbane musings on the contradictions between love and money, faith and fashion, between a child's innocence and a tired planet's anxious future.

Reprinted from Brian D. Johnson, "Flying down to Rio: A pop veteran finds the Brazilian beat," *McLean's*, 12 November 1990, 78.

Topics for Further Investigation

1. Paul Simon and his album "The Rhythm of the Saints"
2. The effect of Hollywood on movies around the world
3. The Grammy^{SM} awards for music
4. Criteria for judging movies and popular music around the world
5. Artistic freedom and censorship: obscene language in pop music
6. What makes a superstar
7. Your favorite musician

Is anyone safe from AIDS? The articles on pages 63 and 65 discuss the rapid spread of AIDS and some of its consequences.

Writing Better Reading Reports

The purpose of this lesson is to give you further guidelines for writing Reading Reports. After practicing writing Reading Reports, you have probably discovered that it is not always easy to decide what to include in your summary section or how to go about writing a response. You will find, however, that it will become easier even though the difficulty of the reading you do increases. More importantly, you will find that you truly understand the reading and are able to use the information in it in a variety of ways.

An important factor in becoming an independent and confident reader is your ability to demonstrate that you understood what you read. One way to do this is to *summarize* the reading. Because a summary contains the main idea and only the essential information in an article, preparing one forces you to analyze a reading by asking what the writer's main point is and what important information is given to develop it. When you have written a summary of an article by expressing in your own words what you have read, you can be sure that you have understood its contents: what is important, and what is merely detail.

Writing a Reading Report Summary

As a general rule, a Reading Report summary should be one or two paragraphs in length. The first sentence of the summary should express the main idea of the reading, and the rest of the summary should include:

1. The major points the writer uses to develop or support the main idea
2. The definitions which are necessary to understand the article
3. The writer's attitude, if one is expressed in the article

The summary should *not* include details or examples that appear in the article unless a general concept cannot be understood without an illustration of what is meant. Of course, the summary should be written in your own words to demonstrate that you have understood the article. You can make use of some of the techniques from Part I to help you paraphrase information from the article. You should *never* copy sentences directly from your reading.

Because a summary is a miniature version of the original reading, you should not express your opinion about the subject matter. You will have the opportunity to do this in the Response section of the Reading Report.

Writing a Response

The Response section of your Reading Report gives you the chance to express your opinions, ideas, or reactions to the information you have acquired in that reading. For example, while reading the article on world music, you might be reminded of some of your favorite music from a foreign country and decide to write a little about it in your response. Or, if you are happy to learn that Third World musicians are becoming popular in the United States, mention it. Avoid responses like "I liked the article" or "I don't agree with the author." If you want to express an opinion about the article, explain why you liked it or why you don't agree. Usually you can do this in one or two sentences, although sometimes you may wish to write more.

In this chapter, you will read two newspaper articles about AIDS. For the first article, a summary has been prepared to demonstrate what a Reading Report summary should be. For the second one, you and your classmates will prepare a summary together, but you will write your own response.

SPECIALIZED VOCABULARY

1. AIDS (Acquired Immune Deficiency Syndrome)—a disease caused by a virus that attacks and destroys the system of the human body that fights disease

2. sub-Saharan—all countries in Africa south of the Sahara Desert

3. heterosexual—characterized by sexual desire for those of the opposite sex

4. HIV—Human Immunodeficiency Virus, which is the virus causing AIDS infection

5. crack cocaine—a less expensive form of cocaine that is smoked

6. human support system—those public services, such as medical care and counseling, that help members of a community to meet their needs

7. homosexual—characterized by sexual desire for those of the same sex

8. lobbying—the act, usually by organized groups or their representatives, of getting or trying to get legislators to vote for or against something

9. intravenous—injecting a substance directly into a blood vein

Sharp Rise in AIDS Infection Is Reported in Third World

Eight to ten million people around the world are now infected with the virus that causes AIDS, and the incidence of the infection is rising dramatically in some parts of the world, the World Health Organization reports.

The estimate is consistent with an earlier projection by the organization that 15 million to 20 million people would be infected by the human immunodeficiency virus by the year 2000.

But the announcement Tuesday said "marked increases" in infections in Asia and Latin America, coupled with an expanding epidemic in sub-Saharan Africa, could force a "dramatic upward revision" of the projections in the next several years. Officials said this was particularly true in Asia, where the agency forecast a million to 1.5 million infections by 2000, but where 500,000 have already occurred.

Rise in Heterosexual Cases

The increases reflect the growing heterosexual transmission of the AIDS virus around the world, the agency said.

"It is now clear that the toll of HIV infection around the globe is worsening rapidly, especially in developing countries," said Dr. Michael H. Merson, the director of the agency's worldwide program on AIDS.

The new estimates are based on a recently completed analysis of blood tests in which the AIDS virus was found in 1988 and 1989. The analysis showed that the rate of HIV infection is slowing in industrialized countries.

But in sub-Saharan Africa, cases of HIV infection have increased to about 5 million from 2.5 million in 1987. That year, most infected people were found in big cities; now the virus is spreading to rural areas. The agency calculated that about one in 40 adult men and women is infected in that region.

Data from Southern Asia, including Thailand and India, showed marked increases in HIV infection among female prostitutes and people who inject drugs into themselves. The total number of HIV infections in Asia has risen from next to nothing two years ago to at least 500,000, the agency reported.

The organization also forecast a rising incidence of HIV infections, AIDS cases and deaths among women and children in the 1990's, with three million of them expected to die in the next decade.

Reprinted from the *New York Times*, 22 August 1990, A18.

Summary:
A recent World Health Organization report states that cases of AIDS infection are increasing rapidly in developing countries, particularly in Asia, Latin America, and sub-Saharan Africa. Currently, the virus has infected 8 to 10 million people. The infection rate in developed countries is not increasing as rapidly as it had been, but the dramatic increase in other parts of the world indicates that by the year 2000 between 15 and 20 million people may suffer from AIDS. Further, the report predicts that AIDS cases will continue to rise among heterosexuals (including women and children) and among those in rural areas of the Third World.

This *New York Times* article contains a lot of information about how AIDS is spreading. On careful reading, however, you can see that the main idea is the rapid and unexpected increase in cases in the developing world. This concept is expressed as the first (and most important) sentence of the summary. Notice the kind of information that has not been included in the summary: statistics about the increase in Asia, how these statistics were arrived at, and data from the 1988 and 1989 reports. These do not have to be included because they are details or examples used to illustrate the main points in the article.

It is also clear that the summary does not use the same words as the original article. Notice how some of the wording has been paraphrased:

1. " . . . rising dramatically . . . " . . . is increasing rapidly . . .

2. " . . . 8 to 10 million people around the world are now infected . . . " Currently, the virus has infected 8 to 10 million people worldwide.

3. " . . . the rate of HIV infection is slowing in the industrialized world." The infection rate in developed countries is not increasing as rapidly as it had been.

You will find that as you practice paraphrasing by writing your Reading Reports, it will become easier for you. The article that follows is also about the spread of AIDS, but the information in it is quite different from that in the first. Read it through completely one time without stopping to look up words, but underline the words you don't know. When you have finished, you will discuss the article with some of your classmates.

Commission Finds Rural AIDS Sufferers Face Discrimination

By Keith Kendrick
Washington Post Staff Writer

According to the stereotype, a portrait of life in American small towns shows a picture of cozy families, kindly neighbors and helpful friends.

But people with AIDS who live in those communities find little more than isolation and terror.

According to the National Commission on AIDS, an official advisory body to the White House and Congress, there is a new epidemic plaguing sufferers of the disease in rural U.S. communities: fear and bigotry.

Fanned by ignorance surrounding HIV infection and AIDS, friends, neighbors and even families turn on sufferers with hostility and discrimination.

Commenting on her investigations, commission member Belinda Ann Mason, a mother of two who was infected with the disease during a blood transfusion, said: "I have seen rural America at its warm, supportive best and at its close-minded, bigoted worst."

Although the epidemic continues to be most severe in urban areas, the number of AIDS cases diagnosed in rural towns across the country has risen by 37 percent in the last year, seven times faster than the 5 percent rate of increase in cities of more than 500,000.

In rural Georgia, for example, the number of cases tripled in the last two years, an increase attributed to the growth of crack cocaine use which has resulted in young women trading sex with multiple partners for drugs or money.

But, despite that growth, health care and human support systems are woefully inadequate, according to the commission, which described them as "unable to serve even their commu-

nity's basic needs, let alone the increase in HIV."

The study, the third to be produced by the 15-member commission since it was set up in November 1988, also concludes that experimental drug-testing includes too few minorities, women and children.

But the report focused mainly on discrimination against AIDS victims by the general public and even by health-care workers.

Ronald L. Jerrell, 25, of Owensboro, Ky., population about 50,000, knows firsthand about that discrimination.

Infected with the disease, "probably through sexual intercourse" with another homosexual, four years ago, Jerrell said he was shunned by the townspeople and was "held at arm's length" by his friends.

"The difference between having cancer and having AIDS is that people bring you flowers and cards when you have cancer. When you have AIDS they don't even visit you," said Jerrell, whose AIDS has destroyed his immune system, causing an eye infection that has left him partially blind.

Jerrell's reaction was not to withdraw from society, but rather to fight by lobbying for more education about AIDS through the Washington-based group, the National Association of People with AIDS.

"Slowly my friends started to come back as I started to convince them that there was nothing to fear from someone who has AIDS," Jerrell said.

But other sufferers in small towns are not so lucky. They experience hostility and bigotry daily, the commission reported. Many lose their jobs: One restaurant manager in Kentucky was

demoted to switchboard operator when his boss found out he had AIDS.

Commission members visited many communities in Georgia, Mississippi, Arkansas and Texas—where they found AIDS education virtually non-existent—and reported similar tales of "bigotry," including a man who was thrown out of church, people losing their jobs and apartments and even sufferers who were rejected by their families.

One man said the fear of being "found out" is so terrifying that he sneaks out to his mother's car at night, covers himself with a blanket and waits for his mother to come out at dawn to drive him many miles to another county where he can receive treatment anonymously.

In addition to its prevalence in rural society, the commission said, discrimination is also rife among medical workers. Many dentists and physicians refuse to treat people infected with HIV, apparently unaware that the virus, spread through blood and semen, is almost exclusively passed on through sex or needle-sharing by intravenous drug users, not by casual contact.

The commission called for a number of measures that could help relieve the problems identified in its report, including the provision of a comprehensive primary health care program, expanded AIDS education initiatives in rural areas and more commitment to improve drug-testing programs.

It also suggests expanding the National Health Service Corps, which sends doctors to rural areas, and other groups to help meet the need for primary health care for rural AIDS patients.

Reprinted from Keith Kendrick, "Commission Finds Rural AIDS Sufferers Face Discrimination," *Washington Post* sec. A. 22 August 1990.

Discussion Questions

1. The second article reports discrimination against people with AIDS. Are AIDS patients discriminated against in your country? If so, in what ways?

2. For many people, AIDS is not only a medical issue but also a moral one. Why is this so? Do you believe that moral judgments can be made about the disease and the people who have it?

3. Even in developed countries, limited money is available for medical research. Do you feel that governments should devote more of their financial resources to finding a cure for AIDS, or do you think that research money should be devoted to finding a cure for other diseases, such as cancer?

4. What is the role of education in trying to control the spread of AIDS? Do you believe that AIDS education should be a part of a high school curriculum, or is this issue too sensitive for young people?

5. How would you react if someone you knew developed AIDS? Would you be afraid to continue to have contact with him or her?

Practice 1

After discussing some of the issues raised in the article, decide which information should be in the first sentence (the main idea) and what important points to include in the summary. When you have agreed on these points, write the summary section of the Reading Report together. When you have completed your summary, you may wish to compare your group's report with those of other groups. Notice the variety of ways in which the information from the article can be paraphrased. Next, each person should fill in the Reading Report Form at the end of this lesson. Fill in the information about the article and check the type of reading. Use the summary your group has prepared, but write your own response.

Practice 2

The following sentences contain key words and phrases from the readings. Paraphrase the parts indicated to show that you understand their meaning. Try to do this without using a dictionary.

1. "Eight to ten million people around the world are now infected with the virus that causes AIDS, and _the **incidence** of the infection is rising_ dramatically in some parts of the world, the World Health Organization reports."

2. "But the announcement Tuesday said 'marked increases' in infections in Asia and Latin America, **coupled with** _an expanding epidemic_ in sub-Saharan Africa, could force a 'dramatic upward revision' of the projections in the next several years."

3. "Officials said this was particularly true in Asia, where _the agency **forecast** a million to 1.5 million infections_ by 2000, but where 500,000 have already occurred."

4. "The total number of HIV infections in Asia _has risen from **next to nothing** two years ago to at least 500,000_, the agency reported."

5. "According to the National Commission on AIDS, an advisory body to the White House and Congress, _there is a new epidemic **plaguing** sufferers of the disease_ in rural U.S. communities: fear and bigotry."

6. "But, despite that growth, health care and _human support systems are **woefully inadequate**_, according to the commission, which described them as 'unable to serve even their community's basic needs, let alone the increase in HIV.'"

7. "One man said that the fear of being 'found out' is so terrifying that he sneaks out to his mother's car at night, covers himself with a blanket and waits for his mother to come out at dawn to drive him many miles to another county where _he can receive treatment **anonymously**_."

8. "The commission called for _a **number of measures**_ that could help relieve the problems identified in its report, including the provision of a comprehensive primary health care program, expanded AIDS education initiatives in rural areas and more commitment to improve drug-testing programs."

Check Your Progress

Look at the following useful words from the readings. If there are any you don't recognize or know how to use, consider adding them to your vocabulary list.

epidemic	calculate	urban
discrimination	stereotype	bigotry
spread	victim	prevalence
estimate	rural	rife
projections		

Practice 3

Bring an article you have chosen and read it to the class. In small groups, discuss the main points and explain the important vocabulary in your article. Following your discussion, write a Reading Report, being sure to follow the instructions in this lesson. Then, exchange Reading Reports with another member of your group. Discuss how you handled paraphrasing, and explain why you included the information you did in your report. Make written suggestions on each other's reports and return them.

Topics for Further Investigation

1. Current research on a cure for cancer
2. Diet as a method of disease prevention
3. Folk cures
4. The common cold
5. Aspirin—the miracle drug
6. Requiring vaccination for children

Name _____

Date _____

READING REPORT

Title _____ Author _____

Name of Publication _____ Number of Pages _____

Date of Publication _____

Type of Reading: _____ Group _____ Personal Interest _____ Academic/Serious

Source of Reading: _____ Chapter in a Book

_____ Newspaper Article

_____ Magazine Type: _____ News _____ Popular _____ Serious

_____ Journal Article

_____ Other _____

SUMMARY

RESPONSE

VOCABULARY

Is it possible to read another person's mind? Learn more about strange phenomena in "The Nature of Parapsychology" on page 72.

Reporting Orally on Your Reading

One of the most enjoyable and exciting results of reading can be to share the new information you have acquired with others. This can be done informally, by talking with friends, or formally, by presenting what you have learned to a group. In this chapter, we will practice the skills necessary to improve your oral reports.

The subject of the readings you will do is paranormal phenomena, that is, events for which there is no reasonable or scientific explanation for what happened. You have probably heard or read about such phenomena. For instance, you may know someone who has had a dream predicting an unlikely event which later happened, or you may have read about doctors who perform operations mentally, without actually cutting into the body. Although there is evidence that many of these things really happened, there is no way we can explain them in terms of accepted scientific principles. This may be the reason why most of us find the paranormal so intriguing and why there is so much interest in and controversy about these events. The article which follows presents an impartial view of such paranormal phenomena.

Many of the words used to describe the paranormal are not common English words, and you will notice that throughout the article there are several definitions. For example, in the second paragraph, the words *parapsychology*, *telepathy*, and *clairvoyance* are defined. Providing definitions within an article is a common practice when the subject is specialized or technical. Other words which are not defined in the text but which you will need to know to understand it are listed below.

SPECIALIZED VOCABULARY

1. supernatural—things that cannot be explained by natural law or forces
2. mesmeric—sleep-like or hypnotic
3. trance—a physically induced state of altered consciousness as in hypnosis
4. medium—a person through whom messages are sent from the dead
5. hauntings (v. to haunt)—the supposed visits to a place by ghosts
6. apparition—the sighting of a ghost or phantom
7. poltergeist—a ghost who is responsible for noisy disturbances
8. anesthesia—a drug used to eliminate pain
9. psychic—beyond known physical processes

The Nature of Parapsychology

by Pat Hyland

Every year, at just about this time, interest in the paranormal heightens. The display of ghostly images and ghost stories peaks with the celebration of Halloween. Age-old questions are raised. Are ghosts real? Can a house be haunted? What causes the inexplicable clangings and bangings heard in the night?

Assuming that for every question, there is an answer, parapsychologists attempt to find the answers to these questions, and others like them, through research. Their field is parapsychology, and it is defined by Webster's Dictionary as "the study that investigates the psychological aspect of apparently supernatural phenomena as telepathy (thought transference), clairvoyance (the power of discerning, while in a mesmeric trance, objects which are not present to the normal senses), extrasensory perception (ESP) and others."

Parapsychologists study two kinds of phenomena: ESP and psychokinesis (PK). ESP refers to gaining information through nonsensory means. For example, you may know before the telephone rings that a close relative is trying to contact you. PK refers to affecting an object at a distance without physical means such as mentally causing a spoon to move or rolled dice to consistently show a predicted number.

Psychical researchers also investigate the human personality's survival after death, and deal with related topics such as trance mediumship, hauntings, apparitions, poltergeists (involuntary PK) and out-of-body experiences. The name of this field of investigation is derived from the Society of Psychical Research, founded in England in 1882 and in the U.S. in 1884. Both groups are still active and publishing their findings.

Early in its history, the British group investigated hypnotism. Considered a radical practice at the time, hypnotism has since been claimed by the fields of medicine and psychology. It is now used to treat a variety of physiological and behavioral problems including the elimination of pain and as a method of control by those who smoke and those who overeat. Some obstetricians have even used it as the sole anesthesia during childbirth.

The British society has also investigated mental (ESP) and physical (PK) phenomena reported at seances (meetings designed to communicate with spirits of those "who have passed from the human stage"), recording what it considered valid paranormal phenomena. One of the earliest records, dated from 1833 to 1836, concerns examinations of the physical medium Daniel Douglas Home by the British chemist and physicist, Sir William Crookes. Their sessions produced paranormal phenomena and were conducted in full light and have never been satisfactorily explained.

In the U.S., the Parapsychology Laboratory of North Carolina's Duke University, which began publishing literature on this subject in the 1930s, was one of the earliest groups to get involved in parapsychology. Their research was directed by the American psychologist, Joseph Banks Rhine. He propelled investigations from isolated and often vague anecdotal reports to a mathematical study, one based on statistics and the law of probability.

During one form of ESP experiment, Rhine and associates used a deck of 25 cards bearing five designs. During testing, if an individual correctly identified five or less of the hidden symbols on 25 cards, the results were attributed to chance. An individual who correctly identified 60 percent or more was considered to have ESP.

In 1965, Rhine retired from Duke University and moved his research to the privately endowed Foundation for Research on the Nature of Man.

Today, parapsychology is a firmly established and broadly recognized area. Independent research centers abound. Among them is the American Society for Psychical Research, formed in 1857. Headquartered in New York City, the organization, whose members include international scholars working in this field, was granted affiliation status in 1969 by the American Association for the Advancement of Science.

Although skeptics might argue that psychic research seems to defy the scientific method, interest remains high. The answers to our many questions which fall into parapsychology's realm may be just around the next research corner.

Reprinted from Pat Hyland, "The Nature of Parapsychology," *Potomac Life*, October 1990, 17.

Discussion Questions

1. Have you or anyone you know well had any paranormal experiences? What happened? Can you think of any way to explain how or why it happened?
2. Have you heard or read about unexplained events other than the kinds mentioned in the article?
3. Do you believe that religion, science, or psychology might offer some explanation for these events?
4. Why do you think scientists are reluctant to accept the paranormal?
5. How are ghosts or "spirits" treated in your culture?

Practice 1

The following sentences from the reading contain key words and phrases. Paraphrase the parts indicated to show that you understand their meaning. Try to do this without using a dictionary.

1. "***Assuming that*** *for every question,* there is an answer, parapsychologists attempt to find the answers to these questions and others like them. . . ."
2. "*ESP* ***refers to*** *gaining information* through nonsensory means."
3. "The name of this field of investigation *is* ***derived from*** the Society of Psychical Research. . . ."
4. "***Considered*** *a radical practice at the time,* hypnotism has since been claimed by the fields of medicine and psychology."
5. "During testing, if an individual correctly identified five or less [*sic*] of the hidden symbols on 25 cards, *the results were* ***attributed to*** *chance.*"
6. "Today, parapsychology is a firmly established and *broadly* ***recognized*** *area.*"
7. "Although skeptics might argue that *psychic research seems to* ***defy*** *the scientific method,* interest remains high."

Check Your Progress

Look at the following useful words from the reading. If there are any you don't recognize or know how to use, consider selecting them to add to your vocabulary list.

heighten	survival	symbol
inexplicable	sole	endowed
apparently	valid	affiliation
affecting	to get involved in	realm
consistently	based on	

Finding Information for an Oral Report

In discussing the paranormal, you have no doubt talked about many interesting things and come up with new ideas in your discussion groups. In your oral reports, you should choose one of the specific subjects which you find particularly interesting. Then, using the *Readers' Guide*, or the *Newspaper Index*, or the card catalog, find an article about that subject. Because the paranormal is a topic that—despite its popular appeal—is not considered truly academic, you may have to use a public library rather than an academic one to find articles about it. After you have located and read your article, write a Reading Report on it. This will help you focus on the main ideas you will choose to include in your oral report.

Preparing for an Oral Report

It is a good idea to use note cards to record the information you will include in your oral report. If you use the Reading Report Form as the basis for your talk, you will be tempted to read rather than speak to your audience. Prepare your notes by using phrases rather than complete sentences to remind you of what you want to say. This will make it easier for you to speak naturally, rather than simply reading. Furthermore, because you want to make your talk interesting, your oral report will include details and examples from the article that are not included in the summary.

Begin with a question, an unusual fact, or anecdote that will arouse the interest of your audience. The questions in the first paragraph of "The Nature of Parapsychology" are a good example of how this can be done. Next, mention the title of the article, the author, and the name of the publication in which you found it. You may want to write this information on the blackboard, along with specialized words from the article that may be unfamiliar to your classmates but important to understanding your report. Do not try to define everything, only the most important words!

The next part of your report should explain the main idea and important supporting information in the article. In other words, it will include the most significant parts of the summary. Don't rewrite the entire summary in your notes. Use important words and phrases to remind you of the points you want to present as you are speaking. In this section, you should also include one or two details or examples from the article which may not be part of your summary, but which you think would be particularly interesting to others.

At the end of your oral report, you will tell your classmates what your response to the article was: whether you agreed or disagreed if the subject is a controversial one; what questions came to your mind after reading it; what it reminded you of; or any personal opinions you may have formed. Be prepared to answer questions about your report when you have finished, but don't be afraid to admit that you don't know the answer or that you would prefer not to answer a particular question.

Following is the summary and response sections from a Reading Report on "The Nature of Parapsychology" and the notes from it that could be used for an oral report.

Summary:
This article describes the kind of research being conducted in parapsychology, which is the field that investigates such unusual events as telepathy (transferring thoughts from one person to another without communication) and ESP (knowledge acquired through other than normal sensory means). Parapsychologists assume that there must be some explanation for these occurrences, and they attempt to find it through scientific study. Serious research on the paranormal began in England in the middle of the 19th century and has continued to the present. One of the best-known American researchers was Joseph B. Rhine, a psychologist, who began mathematical studies of ESP. Although many people do not believe that paranormal phenomena are compatible with scientific research, the American Society for Psychical Research became affiliated with the American Association for the Advancement of Science in 1969.

Response:
I am really interested in finding out more about the paranormal because I know someone who has dreams that frequently predict what actually happens.

1

Interest: Have you ever had the feeling someone far away is trying to contact you or had a dream come true? (discussed in)
Title: "The Nature of Parapsychology"
Author: Pat Hyland
Source: Potomac Life

2

Vocabulary :
   – parapsychology
   – ESP
   – PK   } define
   – telepathy   each
   – clairvoyance
                ↘ write on board

3

Main Idea: describes research
             done in parapsychology
                   ↓ define
  – assume there must be
  explanation
  – use scientific methods

Tips for Giving an Oral Report

1. Practice your presentation, using your notes. If possible, use a tape recorder when you practice so you can listen to the tape to see how well you have done and to determine the time length of your presentation. Your teacher will tell you how long your report should be. If you have trouble pronouncing any words, ask your teacher or an American friend for help before the day of your presentation.

2. Begin by mentioning the title of the article, the author, and the name of the publication. Then, write the words you will define on the blackboard.

3. Speak slowly and loudly enough so that everyone can hear you. If you speak too fast, your audience might miss an important part or misunderstand what you say. If you do not project your voice, only those sitting close to you will be able to hear.

4. Be confident. Relax. Smile. You are speaking from notes about an article that you—not your classmates—have read.

5. Make eye contact with your audience. This gives them the sense of being a part of the presentation and helps to maintain their interest in what you are saying.

6. Keep it simple. Do not be tempted to try to tell *everything* about the article or give lengthy explanations. Do not wander too far from your notes.

7. Hold your notecards comfortably in both hands so that you can easily see the cues and so that your hands are occupied.

8. Do not read from your notes. Try to speak in a normal conversational way. An audience becomes easily bored when someone is reading *at* them.

9. Be thoroughly familiar with the article so that you can answer questions. If you do not know the answer or would prefer not to answer a personal question, say so.

Practice 2

Prepare an oral report on the article you have read on a paranormal phenomenon, using the suggestions in this chapter. Your teacher will assign a date for each member of the class to give a presentation. When you are assigned oral reports in the future, remember to choose to report on an article that you found very interesting. A topic of high interest helps to keep the attention of the audience.

Topics for Further Investigation

1. Witchcraft or shamanism
2. Astrology
3. Handwriting analysis
4. Tarot cards or ouija boards
5. Fortune-tellers
6. The Bermuda Triangle
7. The search for Atlantis

Is abortion ever justified? Read about how the major religions of the world treat this issue in "Faith and Abortion" on pages 82 to 85.

Improving Your Discussion Skills

The article you will read in this chapter, "Faith and Abortion: Where the Major Religions Disagree," may be longer than the articles you have previously read on your own. To help you understand the reading, background information on abortion and a summary of this article are provided for you.

Articles in journals and textbooks frequently have summaries, sometimes called abstracts, at the beginning or the end of the selection. Reading these summaries will help you get an overview of the information contained in the article and will make it much easier for you to understand the main points. We have already discussed techniques for previewing articles, and by now, you should be in the habit of previewing before you read. These techniques are summarized below, along with other suggestions for you to follow when reading longer articles.

Tips for Reading a Long Article

1. Preview the article before reading it. Look at the pictures or the illustrations, and read what is written underneath them.

2. Read the subheadings for each section of the article, and try to decide what the organization of the article is.

3. If there is a summary at the beginning or at the end, read that first.

4. Ask yourself what questions you expect the article to answer, and try to anticipate what the main points will be.

5. Use a highlighter to mark the main ideas as you read.

6. Concentrate on understanding the introduction, which should help you get an overview, and the first sentence of each paragraph.

7. If you don't understand a section, move ahead. The information b4 e b4 there may not be important, or you may be able to figure it out after you have finished the article.

8. Ask yourself to state the main idea of the article in one or two sentences.

9. After your first quick reading, read it a second time, if necessary.

10. When you have finished reading, put the article aside and tell someone else about it.

**SPECIALIZED
VOCABULARY**

1. rape—to force a woman to have sex against her will
2. incest—sex with a member of the family
3. deformity—something wrong with the baby; a physical or mental defect
4. fetus—an unborn baby
5. scripture—the holy writings of a religion, i.e., the Bible, the Koran
6. canon—religious laws
7. conception—the beginning of pregnancy, when the egg is fertilized

Background Information on Abortion

When does life begin? Is it at the moment of conception, or sometime later in the pregnancy? Should governments pass laws prohibiting or regulating abortions, or is this a personal matter for individual decision? These are difficult questions. In the United States, the Supreme Court ruled in 1973 that it was legal for a woman to have an abortion during the first three months of her pregnancy. This decision is called *Roe v. Wade*. In a more recent decision in 1989, however, the Supreme Court ruled in *Webster v. Reproductive Health Services* that state legislatures could pass laws to limit abortions in their states.

Abortion has therefore become a controversial issue in the United States. There are two groups of people who are trying to influence state legislatures: those who are "pro-life" and those who are "pro-choice." The pro-life group wants to prohibit legal abortions, while the pro-choice group wishes to leave the choice up to the individual.

To a large extent, one's view of abortion is a matter of religious belief. In the United States, there are two main religions: Christian and Jewish. The Christian faith includes Catholic, Protestant, and Eastern Orthodox churches. The Protestant branch of the Christian faith has many different churches called "denominations." The major Protestant denominations are Baptist, Methodist, Lutheran, Presbyterian, and Episcopal, but there are many other smaller groups. As you will see, these various Christian churches do not agree on whether abortion is morally right or wrong.

The following article examines the position of the world's major religions on the question of abortion. What do these faiths believe, and why?

Summary of the Article

There is great disagreement among the world's major faiths on the question of abortion. Some religious groups, such as Moslems, allow abortions for any reason during the first 40 days of the pregnancy; others, such as Catholics, believe that life begins at the moment of conception, and therefore abortion is a form of murder. Hindus agree that the soul enters the fetus at the moment of conception, but because they believe in rebirth, Hindus think that the soul will have another chance at life.

Some religious groups base their position on abortion on their holy scriptures, other teachings of their religious leaders, or on church law. Other groups, particularly Protestants, have issued official church positions after their members or governing boards have voted on circumstances when abortion should be permitted. In some cases, religious groups encourage members to be politically active and work toward passing laws regulating abortion. Other groups stress the need to allow for individuals to make up their own minds about abortion, and they believe that the government should not attempt to regulate matters which are really personal and religious.

In determining their stand on abortion, religious faiths must consider circumstances which might justify an abortion. The major reasons for permitting abortions are rape, incest, a threat to the life or health of the mother, or the certainty that the fetus is deformed. All faiths seem to recognize that abortion may be necessary when the life of the mother is threatened, although Catholics would ask the family to choose between the life of the mother and the life of the fetus as if the two lives were equal.

Some religious groups interpret the "health" of the mother as being the mental or spiritual health as well as the physical health. They therefore permit abortion when the mother would suffer psychological damage if she were forced to have the baby. Most faiths believe, however, that it is wrong to have an abortion because having the baby would be inconvenient, or because the parents want to choose the sex of their child.

Note that the important points in the following article have been highlighted.

Faith and Abortion: Where the World's Major Religions Disagree

By Mark Weston

PROTESTANT

Presbyterian Church

The Presbyterian Church, with more than 3 million members, is one of the most strongly pro-abortion rights Protestant denominations. The church filed an amicus curiae brief with the U.S. Supreme Court last fall opposing the state of Missouri in the case of *Webster v. Reproductive Health Services.*

In its brief, the church declared that its General Assembly "has repeatedly affirmed that, although abortion should not be used as a form of birth control, the abortion decision must remain with the individual, must be made on the basis of conscience and personal religious principles and must remain free of governmental interference." The church also argued that "the morality of abortion is a question of stewardship of life and abortion can, therefore, be considered a responsible choice . . . when resources are inadequate to care for a child appropriately."

In June 1989, the 201st General Assembly of the Presbyterian Church reaffirmed these positions.

Southern Baptist Convention

In 1982, the Southern Baptist Convention, the nation's largest Protestant denomination with more than 14.5 million members, resolved "that we support and will work for appropriate legislation and/or constitutional amendment which will prohibit abortions except to save the life of the mother." The Southern Baptists reaffirmed this resolution in 1984 and 1989.

As is true in other Protestant denominations, resolutions of the Southern Baptist Convention are not binding upon any individual Baptist or Baptist church. Nevertheless, the Southern Baptists are strongly antiabortion. Motions to allow rape and incest as exceptions that would justify an abortion were defeated by the Southern Baptist Convention in 1982, 1984 and 1989.

Richard Land, director of the Southern Baptist Christian Life Commission in Nashville, estimates that two-thirds of Southern Baptists favor government action that would restrict or outlaw abortion, but acknowledges that perhaps one-third of Southern Baptists (including former president Jimmy Carter) believe that even if one is personally opposed to abortion, it is not an issue in which the government should involve itself.

Land argues that antiabortion legislation is not an imposition of one group's morality on another, but protects an unborn child from the mother's imposition of her morality on the child.

Like other denominations, Southern Baptists base their views on several Bible verses. One is Jeremiah 1:5, "Before I formed you in the womb I knew you, and before you were born I consecrated you; I appointed you a prophet to the nations." Another verse, Exodus 21:22, is much in dispute. In the Revised Standard Version (and Jewish translations are virtually the same) the verse reads, "When men strive [fight] together, and hurt a woman with child, so that there is a miscarriage, and yet no harm follows, the one who hurt her shall be fined, according as the woman's husband shall lay upon him; and he shall pay as the judges determine. If any harm follows, then you shall give life for life, eye for eye, tooth for tooth."

Many Protestants and Jews point to the relatively light penalty of a fine as biblical authority that an abortion is not a murder, and that the fetus does not have the rights of a human being. But Southern Baptists and other conservative Protestants disagree. They translate the word "miscarriage" as "premature birth." If a baby is born prematurely and "no harm follows," then there is only a fine. But if there is harm—that is, if the unborn baby dies, then it is a murder, and the penalty must be "life for life." So the same Bible verse is cited by clergy on both sides of the abortion question.

United Methodist

The General Conference of the United Methodist Church, the nation's second largest Protestant denomination with more than 9.1 million members, resolved in 1984 and reaffirmed in April 1988, that "our belief in the sanctity of unborn life makes us reluctant to approve abortion. But we are equally bound to respect the sacredness of the life and well-being of the mother, for whom devastating damage may result from an unacceptable pregnancy . . . we recognize tragic conflicts of life with life that may justify abortion, and in such cases we support the legal option of abortion under proper medical procedures. We cannot affirm abortion as an acceptable means of birth control, and we unconditionally reject it as a means of gender selection."

Lutheran

The Evangelical Lutheran Church in America is a new denomination formed by the January 1988 merger of the American Lutheran Church and the Lutheran Church in America, which had directly opposing views on abortion. The church has more than 5.2 million members.

In its first national assembly in August 1989 antiabortion forces objected to a church statement that encouraged "free access" to abortion services. The convention prevented a major confrontation by adopting substitute wording that calls on church leaders to help "couples and individuals explore all issues."

Missouri Synod

As recently as July 13, 1989, the convention of the Lutheran Church, Missouri Synod, with more than 2.6 million members, reaffirmed its longstanding positions that the unborn "are persons in the sight of God from the time of conception," and that "abortion is not a moral option except as a tragically unavoidable byproduct of medical procedures necessary to prevent the death of another human being [such as] the mother." The convention welcomed "the Supreme Court's *Webster* decision as a necessary first step toward the full restoration of the right to life."

Last fall, the Lutheran Church, Missouri Synod, along with the Southern Baptist Convention and the National Association of Evangelicals, filed an amicus curiae brief with the U.S. Supreme Court in support of the state of Missouri in the case of *Webster v. Reproductive Health Services*. In the brief, the churches argued that "no level of inconvenience or discomfort of a human being should be a justification for terminating human life, even at its earliest stages, as is now permitted in the first and second trimesters of pregnancy."

Episcopal

Many of the 2.5 million Episcopalians are active in both the abortion rights and the antiabortion movements. The General Convention in 1988 reflected this division when it opposed "abortion as a means of birth control, family planning, sex selection, or any reason of mere convenience," but also urged "that any proposed legislation on the part of national or state governments regarding abortions must take special care to see that individual conscience is respected, and that the responsibility of individuals to reach informed decisions in this matter is acknowledged and honored."

CATHOLIC

Roman Catholic Church

The position of the Roman Catholic Church, with more than 52 million members in the United States and more than 900 million worldwide, is longstanding and well-known: that life begins at the moment of conception and that abortion is murder.

It is based on biblical verses, on church law from as early as 80 A.D., on the pronouncements of Pope Sixtus V in 1588 and Pope Pius IX in 1869, and most recently on the 1968 encyclical of Pope Paul VI, "Humanae Vitae." In the encyclical, Pope Paul VI declared that "directly willed and procured abortion, even if for therapeutic reasons, [is] to be absolutely excluded as licit means of regulating birth."

A woman who secures a completed abortion is automatically excommunicated under Canon 1398 of the Code of Canon Law, regardless of the stage of pregnancy at the time of her abortion.

According to Father Kevin Hart, Director of Family Life and Worship at the Archdiocese of Washington, D.C., cases of rape, incest or the certainty of deformity cannot justify the killing of a fetus. Only two exceptions exist under Catholic law to the prohibition of abortion. First, if the life of the mother is at stake, then her family may choose which of two equal lives should be saved. Second, if a pregnant woman needs surgery, for example, if she has cancer and needs to have her uterus removed, and if the intention behind the surgery is to restore the health of the mother and not to kill the fetus, then an abortion is justified.

EASTERN ORTHODOX

Greek Orthodox Church

Followers of the Greek Orthodox Church, who number more than 1.9 million, believe that life begins at the moment of conception. According to Bishop Isaiah, Chancellor of the Greek Orthodox Archdiocese of North and South America, which has its headquarters in New York, the best example of the biblical basis for this belief is the Annunciation (Luke 1:31), when the angel Gabriel said to Mary, "And behold, you will conceive in your womb and bear a son, and you shall call his name Jesus."

As early as 375 A.D., Saint Basil said "those who give potions for the destruction of the child conceived in the womb are murderers; as are they who take the poisons which kill the child." Today, Greek Orthodox canons prohibit abortion as the unjust killing of a human being, permissible only when it is necessary to save the life of the mother. But if a woman has an abortion and later sincerely repents of her sin, she can be forgiven and welcomed back into the church.

To those who argue that the fetus in the first few weeks of pregnancy is not a full human being, a Greek Orthodox Christian priest will reply that no one is fully human, but that everyone, from embryo to old man, has the potential to become fully human and achieve union with God.

Russian Orthodox Church

The position of the Russian Orthodox Church, with about 1 million members, is identical to that of the Greek Orthodox Church, according to Eric Weaver, secretary to the Metropolitan of the Syosset, N.Y.-based church. Followers of the Russian Orthodox Church believe that life begins at the moment of conception, and that abortion is never justified except to save the life of the mother.

JEWISH

Reform Judaism

Reform Jews, who number 1.3 million, permit abortion when the life or health of the mother is threatened by pregnancy. But for Reform Jews this exception is so wide that an abortion is permissible even when it is the "spiritual or psychological life" of the
(*continued*)

mother that is threatened, according to Rabbi Joseph Weinberg of the Washington Hebrew Congregation. The decision on abortion is the mother's, and she is entitled to terminate her pregnancy if she feels that is appropriate. Rabbi Weinberg believes that "A mother who does not want her child should not have to bring it to life." He adds that under traditional Jewish law, a life is not considered separate from the mother until its head is out of the womb.

In 1981, the Biennial Convention of the Union of American Hebrew Congregations reaffirmed its "strong support for the right of a woman to obtain a legal abortion on the constitutional grounds enunciated by the Supreme Court in its 1973 decision," and opposed "attempts to restrict the right to abortion through constitutional amendments. To establish in the Constitution the view of certain religious groups on the beginning of life . . . would undermine constitutional liberties which protect all Americans."

Conservative Judaism

The Conservative Jewish view of abortion is far closer to that of Reform Judaism than it is to Orthodox Judaism. Although many of the more than 1.2 million Conservative Jews are anti-abortion, many more are pro-abortion rights, according to Rabbi Jack Moline of the Agudas Achim Synagogue in Alexandria. Rabbi Moline says that he opposes government restrictions on a woman's right to have an abortion because he does not want "a conflict between good citizenship and an interpretation of God's will."

In general, Rabbi Moline says, Conservative Jews interpret the Halakha (the body of Jewish law that begins with the Talmud) a little bit more strictly than Reform Jews do. For example, Rabbi Moline does not favor abortions in the case of rape, incest or the certainty of fetal deformity unless the health of the mother is jeopardized by the pregnancy. But like Reform Jews, Rabbi Moline interprets the "health" of the mother to include her mental health and well-being. So if the carrying of a child resulting from a

rape were going to harm the psychological health of a mother, then an abortion would be permissible.

Orthodox Judaism

According to Rabbi Hillel Klaven of the Ohev Sholom in Washington, Orthodox Jews, who number about 1 million, are against abortion except in cases where the life or health of the mother is in jeopardy. Rape, incest or the certainty of a child's deformity are not permissible exceptions to the prohibition against abortion, and cases concerning the physical health of the mother are usually interpreted strictly. Still, circumstances can sometimes justify an abortion. For example, if a woman runs a risk of a permanent and serious disability should her pregnancy continue, then many Orthodox rabbis will allow her to have an abortion.

Although most Orthodox Jews oppose abortion, a sizeable number are also against any government interference in what they see as a religious matter.

MOSLEM

Islam

Moslems, with more than 2.6 million followers in North America and 860 million worldwide, allow abortion for any reason in the first 40 days of pregnancy, but do not permit any afterward, according to Muhammad Aglan, a professor of Koranic jurisprudence at Imam Muhammad ibn-Saud University at Riyadh, Saudi Arabia.

The one exception is when it is necessary to save the life of the mother. A doctor must certify that an abortion is indeed the only way to save the life, according to Aglan. Rape and incest are not exceptions, he said, but the case of deformity in the fetus is a new issue for Moslem scholars to examine.

The scriptural basis for the choice of 40 days comes not from the Koran, which Moslems believe to be the word of God, but from the Hadith, the sayings of Muhammad, which were collected by a scholar named al-Bukhari in the ninth century. Muhammad described the fetus as being "40 days in

the form of seed, then he is a clot of blood for a like period, then a morsel of flesh for a like period, then [at 120 days] there is sent to him the angel who blows the breath of life into him."

Some Moslems believe that abortions can be performed as late as 120 days into pregnancy, Aglan said, but they are a small minority. Most Moslem scholars agree on 40 days as a dividing line between legal and illegal abortions, since the actual number of days after the beginning of a pregnancy is difficult to determine. (About 50.3 percent of U.S. abortions are performed within six weeks, or 42 days, of conception, according to the Alan Guttmacher Institute in New York, which studies and promotes birth and population control.)

EASTERN

Hinduism

There are more than 735 million Hindus worldwide. It is the view of every sect of Hinduism that the soul enters the fetus at the moment of conception, said Seshagir Rao, a professor of religious studies at the University of Virginia. Therefore, traditional Hinduism does not permit abortion except in the cases of rape, incest, and to save the life of the mother.

In modern practice, however, abortion in India today is legal and widely accepted. Under the Medical Termination of Pregnancy Act of 1971, abortion in India is available to women even "in cases of contraceptive failure." Despite the Hindu doctrine against abortion, there is no opposition to legalized abortion from any major political party or group of Hindu priests.

There are two main reasons for this widespread acquiescence to abortion. First, India's population has tripled since World War II and is now well over 800 million. Second, as is true in Buddhist nations, abortion is not an inflammatory issue in India because Hindus, like Buddhists, believe in rebirth, so an abortion does not deprive a conscious entity of its only chance at life.

Sikhism

Sikhs, with more than 16.6 million followers worldwide, are divided on the question of abortion, but the issue is not the burning controversy among Sikhs that it is among Westerners. Although Sikhs are monotheistic, they also believe in rebirth, so an abortion is not necessarily the end of life for a soul.

Scholars agree that the Sikh holy scripture, the Guru Granth Sahib, is silent on abortion and miscarriage. However, the scripture does say that "God sees man from the pit of the womb," and it also states that the purpose of human life is to have the chance to meet God. Some Sikhs, such as Gurpal Bhuller, a physician in Hopewell, Va., conclude from this that abortion is wrong. For "to deny someone a human existence is to deny him a chance to discover God."

Nevertheless, Bhuller allows for exceptions in the cases of rape, incest and when the life of the mother is in jeopardy.

Other Sikhs, especially younger Sikhs, draw upon their religion's ancient tradition of women's rights, and agree with Inderjit S. Sekhon, a priest at the Guru Nanak Foundation of America in Silver Spring, who says that the decision to have an abortion "is the choice of the family involved."

Buddhism

Buddhists, with more than 100,000 followers in the United States and more than 300 million worldwide, are as divided as Christians on the subject of abortion. But it is not the burning issue in Buddhism that it is in Christianity because of the Buddhist belief in rebirth. A Buddhist does not believe that an abortion robs an unborn being of its one and only chance at life. Rather an abortion is more akin to a match, which having failed to light a candle, may yet light another.

Nevertheless, many Buddhists, such as Bhante Gunaratana, a priest at the Bhavana Society in Highview, W. Va., believe that consciousness arises at the moment of conception, and that abortion is a killing and is wrong. Gunaratana favors government laws that prohibit abortion and allow no exceptions except possibly the life of the mother.

Other Buddhists, such as Kenryu T. Tsuji, a priest at the Ekoji Buddhist Temple in Springfield, believe that the decision is one that a woman must decide for herself. While Tsuji acknowledges that all killing is evil, including the killing of insects and flowers, he emphasizes that the situation surrounding each pregnancy is different, and that there can be no rigid rules.

In Japan, a nation that is both Buddhist and Shinto, abortion is extremely common, available on demand and not opposed by any major political parties. Moreover, in the last 20 years, the Buddhist clergy in Japan has created a new rite for aborted fetuses called "Mizuko Kuyo," to relieve the anxiety of women who have had abortions, according to Gary Ebersole, director of religious studies at Ohio State University.

Zen Buddhism

According to Jiro Sensei, a Zen teacher at the Kashain Zendo in Washington, a decision on abortion cannot be dictated by others. The actual decision is not as important to a follower of Zen as the process of the decision-making itself. "A decision should be made in full awareness of its consequences, and should be made by the individual with a clear head, fully wide awake to the whole issue. Because if it is made by a person who is awake, he or she can live with the decision."

Shintoism

The Shinto religion, with more than 100 million followers, has no position on abortion, according to Ohio State's Ebersole, and most Japanese believe that the abortion decision is a personal rather than a governmental matter.

Masato Kawahatsu, a Shinto priest of the Konkoyo sect at the Konkoyo Shrine in San Francisco, agrees that the decision is personal rather than a governmental matter. He believes a pregnant woman and her priest should make the decision together, with the priest acting as a mediator between her personal concerns and the Divine Will.

Mark Weston is a freelance writer in Armonk, N.Y.

Reprinted from Mark Weston, "Faith and Abortion: Where the World's Major Religions Disagree," *Washington Post*, 23 January 1990, Health section.

Language for Clarification and for Disagreement

In discussing sensitive and controversial issues such as abortion and religious beliefs, it is important to be respectful of others' opinions. It is easy for misunderstandings to occur, and it may be necessary to ask someone to explain a statement. To ask for clarification, you might say one of the following:

1. Let me see if I understand that. You said . . .
2. What you're saying is . . .
3. I'm not sure I follow (or understand) what you're saying.
4. I'm sorry. I didn't get what you said about the . . .
5. Could you explain some more about the . . .
6. What did you mean when you said . . .

In your discussion you may wish to disagree with what is being said and present an opposing opinion. Here are some polite phrases which are appropriate to use to disagree and express your own views:

1. That may be true, but . . .
2. You may be right, but . . .
3. I'm not sure that I can agree. Perhaps . . .
4. Well, that could be, but have you considered that . . .
5. I don't know about that, but the article I read said . . .
6. My experience has been different. I think that . . .
7. Perhaps so, but in my opinion . . .
8. On the other hand, it could be that . . .
9. That's an interesting point, but . . .

Questions for Discussion

1. When do you think life begins?
2. What does your religion say about abortion?
3. Is abortion legal in your country? Under what circumstances?
4. Would you advise a woman who had been raped to have an abortion?
5. Concerning abortion laws, do you make a distinction between what is right for you or your family and what others might be allowed to do? Under what circumstances should abortion be permitted:
   - rape?
   - incest?
   - threat to mother's life?
   - threat to mother's health (physical, psychological)?
   - certainty of deformity?
   - economic problems?
   - choosing the sex of the child?
   - pregnant unmarried teenager?

Practice 1

Work with a partner and prepare a response to one of these questions:

1. What is the position of your religion on abortion?
2. What is your position on abortion?

As you discuss with your partner, each of you should ask a question of clarification. If you disagree with something your partner says, practice using one of the phrases to present a different opinion.

Practice 2

The following sentences contain key words and phrases from the reading. Paraphrase the parts indicated to show that you understand their meaning. Try to do this practice without using a dictionary.

1. " . . . although abortion should not be used as a form of birth control, the abortion decision must remain with the individual, must be made *on the basis of **conscience*** and personal religious principles and must remain free of governmental interference."

2. "First, if *the life of the mother is **at stake***, then her family may choose which of two equal lives should be saved."

3. " . . . if the ***intention*** *behind the surgery* is to restore the health of the mother and not to kill the fetus, then an abortion is justified."

4. "Today, Greek Orthodox canons prohibit abortion as the unjust killing of a human being, ***permissible*** *only when it is necessary to save the life of the mother*."

5. "But if a woman has an abortion and later sincerely ***repents*** *of her sin*, she can be forgiven and welcomed back into the church."

6. "The decision on abortion is the mother's, and she is ***entitled*** *to terminate her pregnancy* if she feels that it is appropriate."

7. "For example, Rabbi Moline does not favor abortions in the cases of rape, incest or the certainty of fetal deformity unless *the health of the mother is **jeopardized** by the pregnancy*."

8. "Still, *circumstances can sometimes **justify*** *an abortion*. For example, if a woman runs a risk of a permanent and serious disability should her pregnancy continue, then many Orthodox rabbis will allow her to have an abortion."

9. " . . . Hindus, like Buddhists, believe in rebirth, so an abortion does not ***deprive*** *a conscious entity of its only chance at life*."

Check Your Progress

Look at the following useful words from the reading. If there are any you don't recognize or know how to use, consider adding them to your vocabulary list.

denomination	restrict	conservative
gender	prohibit	interference
morality	oppose	outlaw (v.)
pro-, anti-	favor	

Writing Reading Reports for Longer Articles

Because you may not have done a Reading Report Form for a longer reading selection, the following summary has been done on "Faith and Abortion" to show you how a long article may be handled.

Title: "Faith and Abortion: Where the World's Major Religions Disagree"

Author: Mark Weston

Source: *Washington Post*, January 20, 1990, Health section

Number of Pages: 4

Type of Reading: Newspaper

Summary:

The major religions of the world have very different positions on the question of if and when abortions should be permitted. This article examines the position of the Christian, Jewish, Moslem, Hindu, and Buddhist faiths on the difficult question of abortion.

Some religions, such as the Catholic faith, believe life begins at the moment of conception, while others, such as the Hindu faith, assert that it occurs sometime later in the pregnancy. Some factors which may justify an abortion are rape, incest, a threat to the mother's life or health, or the certainty of deformity.

There is, however, no agreement among the religious faiths as to the circumstances—if any—under which abortions should be permitted and whether or not they should be regulated by the government. Catholics believe that abortion is never justified, while Protestants are divided on the issue. Some Jewish and Moslem groups would permit abortion under certain circumstances, while others would not. The same is true of the Hindus and Buddhists. Most would agree, however, that abortions should always be permitted to save the life of the mother, but never to choose the sex of the baby or just for the convenience of the parents.

Practice 3

Write your own response to complete this Reading Report.

Planning and Participating in Group Discussions

By now you have participated in a number of small group discussions. Let us now look at how you can plan a good discussion around a topic your group chooses to investigate and how you can improve your discussion skills.

When you divide into small groups for discussion, you will first decide on your topic and how to approach it. For example, if your topic is crime, will you focus on a certain aspect of crime such as drug-related crime, murder, burglary, crime in big cities or small towns, crime prevention, punishment, law enforcement, or crime in certain countries? You may wish to divide up the task so that each person reports on a different aspect of the topic in order to have an overview. Or, you may choose to have everyone look for articles on the same aspect to get as much information as possible and to explore the issue in more depth.

Everyone will then do library research to find an appropriate article on the agreed-upon topic. If, however, the topic is a current event, each member of the group may wish to read a different newspaper or news magazine to get information. In either case, the group should ask a question or questions to be answered by the reading and discussion. What information do you wish to know?

On or before the day of the group discussion, the group will select one person to be the group leader and another to be the reporter, who will take notes on the discussion. The group leader will report on the group discussion to the rest of the class, while the reporter will complete the Group Discussion Report Form.

Each person will take a turn presenting his or her article to the group, taking about five minutes each. Do not exchange articles and read them in the group. Instead, summarize and paraphrase the most interesting facts in the article. Make notes for this presentation so it will be clear and well organized. Members of the group should ask questions to clarify any points which are not clear.

After the individual presentations, the group will discuss the topic and prepare the Group Discussion Report Form, which will be submitted to the teacher after the group report is made to the rest of the class. During the discussion, the group leader plays an important role. The leader should guide the discussion, making sure that:

1. All group members have the chance to express their opinions.
2. No one dominates the discussion.
3. Everyone understands what is said.
4. Group members are polite and respectful of each other's opinions.
5. The group stays on the topic and does not begin to talk about other things.
6. The reporter takes good notes in order to (a) report on the discussion to the rest of the class, and (b) prepare the Group Discussion Report Form.

After the discussion, the leader should go over the main points of the presentation with the group to be certain that everyone is satisfied with what he or she will say. During the report to the class, members of the group should feel free to add to what the leader is saying. This should be an informal process.

GROUP DISCUSSION REPORT FORM

Names of Students   Names of Articles

_____

_____

_____

_____

_____

Summary of Discussion:

Questions Raised:

The reporter, who is preparing the Group Discussion Report Form, should read the information on the form to the group to see if they agree. The group leader makes sure that everyone is satisfied with the report. The report lists the names of the group members, the titles of the articles they have read, a summary of the points covered in the discussion, and questions which arose.

Practice 4

Plan a group discussion on a topic of interest to your group. Decide how to approach the topic, do the necessary library research, report on your articles, and hold your discussion. Follow the guidelines in this lesson, and try to practice clarifying and disagreeing, using the language that has been suggested.

Topics for Further Investigation

1. Unmarried teenage mothers and their babies
2. Test-tube babies
3. Birth control
4. Choosing the sex of a baby
5. Adoption

Advanced Activities for Improving Reading, Speaking, and Writing Skills

Whose rights should be protected, smoker's or nonsmokers'? The articles on pages 96 to 100 present both sides of this controversy.

Evaluating What You Read

You have probably already read a number of articles about controversial subjects, including "the right to die" and "abortion" in this book. You have no doubt found from your discussions with your classmates that there are a variety of reactions to such subjects. Individuals tend to make judgments on controversial subjects based on their knowledge about the issue and, more importantly, on their own system of values.

The Writer's Purpose

Writers are aware that some of their readers may know very little about their subject. When the writer's purpose is to *inform*, as in the article on abortion, information on how major religions regard this issue is presented in a direct and factual manner. The author is not making a judgment about which approach is best, nor is he trying to influence your own judgment.

When the writer's purpose is to *persuade*, however, information on a subject is presented in such a way that it will influence the reader to accept the viewpoint of the writer or to alter the reader's previously formed opinions. In fact, many articles, such as newspaper editorials and opinion columns, have just that purpose. Although it is possible to present an argument in a purely objective yet convincing way, some of these articles are written to appeal to emotions rather than to rational analysis.

In order to make educated decisions about the validity of the material you are reading, you need to know what the purpose of the article is. This is not always easy to determine because a writer may not state the purpose directly. Further, writers who wish to convince sometimes use special persuasive techniques which you may be unaware of. Methods of influencing readers' opinions include: mixing facts with opinions, choosing words with positive or negative emotional content, and using faulty logic. "Scare tactics" appeal to the emotions and attempt to frighten. Frequently, these techniques are combined. If you are aware of these devices and learn to recognize them, you will be better able to evaluate the articles you read.

One subject that generates strong reactions in the United States is smoking. While most people agree that the health of the smoker is negatively affected by this habit, there is controversy about whether environmental tobacco smoke (ETS) can harm nonsmokers and whether smoking should be restricted in public places such as offices and restaurants. This issue involves a conflict between the rights of individuals: the rights of nonsmokers to healthy surroundings, and the rights of smokers to personal freedom to do as they wish. The two articles that follow present both sides of this debate. Both articles are intended to persuade.

SPECIALIZED VOCABULARY

1. ETS (environmental tobacco smoke)—smoke that nonsmokers are exposed to in public places, which may affect their health
2. preemption—in this case, one law would be given preference over another, making it impossible for a local law to be more severe than a state law
3. statute—a law
4. Surgeon General—the chief medical officer in the United States government
5. nuisance laws—laws that deal with details or personal matters and therefore irritate both the public and law enforcement officers
6. citation—a summons to appear before a court
7. ordinance—a local law or regulation
8. private sector—non-government businesses
9. a press release—a statement issued by an organization or individual for publication

FOR RELEASE:
TUESDAY, FEBRUARY 28, 1989

ALBANY, NY (February 28, 1989)—A citizens coalition of health, local government, consumer, and environmental groups endorsed legislation introduced today by Governor Mario M. Cuomo to control smoking in public places and in the workplace.

"New York State Association of Counties supports the Governor's proposed legislation, which includes provisions for maintaining the counties' ability to adopt their own smoking restrictions," declared Edwin Crawford, Executive Director, New York State Association of Counties.

"We are pleased that the Governor's anti-smoking proposal will leave the City's strong law intact," said New York City Mayor Edward Koch. "The City's Clean Indoor Air Act is working well. As a result, I believe every New Yorker will live longer, healthier lives. We hope this proposal, when law, will help clear the air in public places across the State," Koch added.

"We strongly support the proposal unveiled today by the Governor. It represents the progress made in last year's negotiations," said John Bullis, Chairman of the New York State Coalition on Smoking Or Health.

"The debate ought not be clouded with tobacco industry tactics designed to strip local governments of their basic ability to protect their citizens. Over the years the tobacco industry has attempted to raise false fears and generate obstructionist issues—such as preemption—to block attainment of a healthy public indoor environment. It is time for our elected representatives to rebuff the cigarette lobby and approve a comprehensive statewide smoking control law," Bullis concluded.

The Governor's bill would provide minimal health-based restrictions on smoking in public places, restaurants, and in places of employment while not preempting local governments that have or may wish to have smoking laws that go beyond state law. In negotiations during the 1988 legislative session, preemption became the major obstacle to passage of a smoking control proposal.

"As we observe the 25th anniversary of the Surgeon General's report, overwhelming scientific and medical evidence has conclusively shown the disastrous and tragic effects of tobacco smoking in America. We applaud the Governor for his commitment for tight smoking restrictions protecting nonsmokers from involuntary exposure to tobacco smoke in places of business, restaurants and other indoor areas where citizens' right to clean air may be violated," said Dr. Pascoe J. Imperato, Editor of the New York State Medical Journal, published by the Medical Society of the State of New York.

"This kind of governmental support will go a long way in protecting New Yorkers, and the Governor's effort should be commended and encouraged not only by the medical profession, but by the community at large," Dr. Imperato continued.

"NYS Association of County Health Officers supports the Governor's Program Bill. Members of NYSACHO regard this proposal as a very substantial step forward to protect public health and set new standards of behavior regarding smoking. We particularly support those provisions of the governor's bill which will permit localities to enact even stronger measures to protect their residents when the need is present," said Dr. William Gratton, Albany County Commissioner of Health and Representative of NYSACHO.

"This is the year for the governor and the legislature to prove they're serious about drug use by limiting exposure to killer tobacco, the most lethal and addictive drug available today," said Blair Horner, New York Public Interest Research Group.

"Most environmental problems are intractable and will take years to resolve. Preventing the harmful effects of tobacco in indoor environments is, however, one major problem that the Legislature can and should resolve in 1989," said Lee Wasserman, Executive Director, Environmental Planning Lobby.

"Any state law should set a basic standard of protection and offer local governments the option to adopt more stringent smoking control laws, just as federal environmental laws allow greater protective standards by state/local governments," stated Andreé Marr, League of Women Voters.

PARTICIPATING GROUPS

New York State Coalition on Smoking OR Health
   American Lung Association
   American Heart Association
   American Cancer Society
New York State Association of Counties
The City of New York
Medical Society of the State of New York
New York State Association of County Health Officials
New York League of Women Voters
New York Public Interest Research Group
Environmental Planning Lobby
American Red Cross in New York State
New York State Public Health Association

Reprinted from a press release by the New York State Coalition on Smoking or Health, 28 February 1989.

Let's set the record straight . . .

Public smoking—common sense for the common good

Have you heard the one about the airline counter agent who asks the passenger whether he'd like a seat in the smoking section—or one *inside* the plane?

It may have been funny the first time a stand-up comedian told it. But it's really no joke. Restrictive smoking laws and regulations have sprouted up across the country for all sorts of places, from airplanes and jury rooms to restaurants and office buildings.

But how far should government go in controlling the personal behavior and restricting the freedom of choice of adults? Must common sense, good manners and mutual consideration be supplanted by statute? Need the freedoms of many be abridged by law to relieve the few of occasional minor annoyances? Let's take a look.

Those who argue for smoking laws often cite health fears to support their views. But these are theories only. The Surgeon General has said there is not sufficient evidence to conclude that other people's smoke causes disease in nonsmokers. The Surgeon General also says no tobacco smoke allergy has been demonstrated in humans. He says what response does occur in healthy nonsmokers may be due to psychological factors.

So when the anti-smokers' health claims are shown to be unproved, the public smoking question boils down to this: Why should it be the business of government?

We think it is *not* the province of government, but of *people*, to work out solutions to problems of social behavior. State interference in such matters is neither effective nor appropriate.

Public smoking laws have been described as nuisance laws.

Dr. Theodore Gill, a dean of John Jay College of Criminal Justice, has written that nuisance laws are "inflicted" by single-minded persons who look to government to solve personal differences—with at least one result they do not anticipate.

"It would be inaccurate and foolish for me to suggest," said Dr. Gill, "that nuisance laws are primary causes for the [increasing] disrespect for the law. I think it accurate though to say such laws contribute to a general disrespect for all law."

He added that in touchy areas such as smoking, involving personal taste, the feelings of others and complex counterclaims of private and public space, "community acceptance and what we hope will be increasingly common courtesy should prevail."

Dr. Gill is right. Common courtesy *should* prevail. Do we really need policemen checking smoking compliance in restaurants, on airplanes, in our office buildings? Of course not.

Most businesses will see to the mutual comfort of smoking and nonsmoking patrons should they perceive the need. Their desire to maximize patronage and profits is the incentive. Proprietors don't need smoking laws. They don't need the police to enforce what they can work out for themselves.

In fact, some businessmen believe such laws could put them out of business. As a Santa Monica restauranteur put it, "If they came in and told me I could allow smoking in [only] one section, and nonsmoking in another . . . I couldn't operate. It wouldn't be economically feasible for me to run my restaurant."

(*continued*)

The police don't want smoking laws either. "We've got enough problems catching holdup men and burglars," was the way Undersheriff Tom Rosa of Santa Clara, California, put it. He was echoed by Assistant Police Chief Michael Sgobba of San Diego, who said, "Unless an officer has absolutely nothing to do, he isn't going to go out and give someone a citation for smoking in an unauthorized zone."

But not just proprietors and law officers feel this way. Eight times in five years electorates—from tiny Zephyrhills, Florida, to San Francisco, *twice* statewide in California—have been able to vote on whether they wanted smoking laws.

16 million ballots later . . .

Eight times average citizens weighed government intervention in public smoking against freedom and self-determination. In all, almost 16 million ballots. And the *vote was for freedom of choice*.

The lone exception was San Francisco. By less than 1 percent of votes cast, the City by the Bay affirmed an ordinance forcing all *private sector* employers to adopt smoking policies agreeable to all *nonsmoking* employees. If a single nonsmoker objects to the policy, the employer must prohibit smoking or face up to $500 in fines daily.

As opposing citizens groups fought a press release battle right up to the November 1983 election in San Francisco, a city council across the country was taking a more reasonable course. Ormond Beach, Florida, city council decided against an ordinance or a ballot question, agreed instead to reject an American Lung Association petition to ban smoking in most public places and to let individual businessmen experiment with smoking policies of their own.

"Municipal nanny"

In San Francisco, columnist Herb Caen quoted one cigar-smoking boss' threat to hire only smokers from now on and the Sunday Examiner & Chronicle editorialized sadly about "the municipal nanny." USA Today wrote that "the emerging conflict creates a serious hazard in the workplace, turning worker against worker."

But in Florida, Daytona Beach News-Journal editors could approve the decision of the city fathers in neighboring Ormond that accommodation is preferable to laws.

"Instead of going overboard on anti-smoking laws or on litigation to kill such laws," wrote the Daytona Beach Evening News, "sensible people will work with each other to resolve smoking disputes amicably and to do so without bringing in government, the police or the courts."

Smokers and nonsmokers, we hope, will continue living and working together as they have for generations, without laws. They know that life is a matter of give and take.

And a smoker knows when it is appropriate to light up. Most are courteous enough to refrain voluntarily when it's obvious they might be bothering others. Most smokers will be accommodating and reasonable.

After all, consideration of the other fellow underlies all our interaction, at work or at play. Or it *should*.

Common sense, above all

Common sense tells us not to raise our voices in a restaurant or a busy office. It tells us not to bathe in heavy perfume or overdo the garlic before going to the movies, not to let our kids run up and down supermarket aisles.

Common sense tells us that cooperation and mutual understanding—respect for the preferences and sensitivities of others—are the simplest and least intrusive means by which smokers and nonsmokers can continue to get along.

Common sense about public smoking is for the common good. Like the Golden Rule. And it might even assure that no one will have to ride *outside* the plane.

For further information on this or any other aspect of the controversies surrounding tobacco and its use, call or write The Tobacco Institute.

 The Tobacco Institute
1875 I Street Northwest
Washington, D.C., 20006
202/457-4800

Reprinted from "Public smoking—common sense for the common good," The Tobacco Institute.

Discussion Questions

1. What is the general attitude towards smokers in your country? Why do you think smoking is such a controversial subject in the U.S.?

2. Do you smoke? If so, why did you begin to smoke? If not, why?

3. Even though most smokers are aware of the harmful effects of tobacco, they continue to smoke. What are some of the reasons for this?

4. Do you believe that there should be restrictions placed on smoking in public places?

5. When someone's smoking bothers you, do you ask him or her to stop? How?

Practice 1

The following sentences contain key words and phrases from the readings. Paraphrase the parts indicated to show that you understand their meaning. Try to do this without using a dictionary.

1. "But how far should government go in controlling the personal behavior and **restricting** *the freedom of choice* of adults?"

2. "Those who argue for smoking laws often **cite** *health fears* to support their views."

3. "Most businesses will see *to the* **mutual** *comfort* of smoking and nonsmoking patrons should they perceive the need."

4. "If they came in and told me I could allow smoking in (only) one section, and nonsmoking in another . . . I couldn't operate. It wouldn't be *economically* **feasible**."

5. "Eight times average citizens weighed government intervention in public smoking against freedom and self-determination. ***In all***, almost 16 million ballots."

6. "As we observe the 25th anniversary of the Surgeon General's report, overwhelming scientific and medical *evidence has* **conclusively shown** the disastrous and tragic effects of tobacco smoking in America."

7. "This kind of governmental support will go a long way in protecting New Yorkers, and the governor's effort *should be* **commended** and encouraged not only by the medical profession, but by the community at large."

8. "Members of NYSACHO **regard** *this proposal* as a very substantial step forward to protect public health and set new standards of behavior **regarding** smoking."

9. "Any state law should set a basic standard of protection and *offer local governments the* **option** *to* adopt more stringent smoking control laws, just as federal environmental laws allow greater protective standards by state/local governments," stated Andreé Marr, League of Women Voters."

Check Your Progress

Look at the following useful words from the readings. If there are any you don't recognize or know how to use, consider adding them to your vocabulary list.

READING 1

legislation	comprehensive	substantial
provision	anniversary	negotiations
intact	overwhelming	obstacle
represent	disastrous	violate
tactics	go a long way	intractable
attainment	at large	

READING 2

regulation	perceive	ban
sufficient	prohibit	courteous
evidence	intervention	common sense
interference	self-determination	controversy
prevail	ballot	assure

The Source

Your first consideration in evaluating a reading should be the source of the article. If a reading is found in an encyclopedia or a textbook, you can be relatively sure that the information is strictly factual. Other sources must be evaluated more carefully.

Here, for example, the first article, a press release from the New York State Coalition on Smoking, appeared in a document entitled "TURNING THE TABLES: How to Beat the Tobacco Industry at Its Own Game" published by an organization called Tobacco-Free America. The second article was prepared by the Tobacco Institute, a group of cigarette manufacturers and tobacco growers. In both cases, the sources clearly indicate the orientation of the articles. You can easily predict the purpose of both articles by identifying their sources. However, many articles that appear in newspapers and magazines also attempt to convince, and the publication itself does not always give you a clue as to the article's purpose.

Fact versus Opinion

Most readings contain both facts and opinions, and because readers want to know how a writer feels about a subject, this is acceptable when the writer identifies an opinion as such. A fact is something that can be proven true or false by checking a reliable source. In the first article, for instance, the phrase "As we observe the 25th anniversary of the Surgeon General's report . . . " can be verified by checking the date of this report. The quote from former New York City Mayor Edward Koch, "The City's Clean Indoor Air Act is working well," is an opinion. It would be very difficult to determine how well this law is working. There is no one source that could be checked to verify this statement.

Practice 2

Look at these quotes from the readings. Try to determine whether they are facts or opinions. Keep in mind that information can be presented as factual but may not be true. If it is something you can verify as true or false by checking a reliable source, identify it as a fact. Also remember that opinions are statements that cannot be proven, even if the author does not identify the statement as an opinion.

1. "The Surgeon General has said there is not sufficient evidence to conclude that other people's smoke causes disease in nonsmokers."
2. "I think it accurate though to say such laws contribute to a general disrespect for all law."
3. "Most environmental problems are intractable and will take years to resolve."
4. "And a smoker knows when it is appropriate to light up."
5. "This kind of governmental support will go a long way in protecting New Yorkers, and the Governor's effort should be commended and encouraged not only by the medical profession, but by the community at large."
6. "Public smoking laws have been described as nuisance laws."

Word Choice

Many words carry two levels of meaning: their actual meaning, as found in a dictionary (denotation), and their emotional content (connotation). Writers are very much aware of both levels of meaning. When they are trying to persuade, they may choose words that they know carry a negative or a positive emotional meaning. You should be aware of the powerful effect word choice can have.

For instance, in the first article, we find "Over the years the tobacco industry has *attempted* to raise *false fears* . . . to block attainment of a *healthy* public indoor environment." The author has used the verb *attempt* to suggest that the tobacco industry has not necessarily been successful in its efforts. The phrase *false fears* is used to indicate that there is no basis for being afraid, and the word *healthy* has been selected because, of course, everyone wants good health.

Further, the second writer asks, "Need the *freedoms* of many be abridged by law to relieve the few of *occasional minor annoyances*?" The word *freedom* has strong emotional meaning, especially for Americans, who consider freedom not only as desirable but also as a right guaranteed them in their Constitution. The dictionary meaning of *annoyance* is an irritation or a bother, suggesting that this is not a serious problem. The adjectives *occasional* and *minor* suggest infrequent and without importance. Clearly, the author wants to convey the idea that the issue is something that seldom occurs but when it does, it is so unimportant, compared to our personal rights, that it should be ignored. The words have been precisely chosen to convey this meaning.

Practice 3

In the following quotes, try to identify those words the writers have selected to use to help convince their readers. Why do you think the writer chose them?

1. " . . . has written that nuisance laws are 'inflicted' by single-minded persons who look to government to solve personal differences . . . "

2. "This is the year for the governor and the legislature to prove they're serious about drug use by limiting exposure to killer tobacco, the most lethal and addictive drug available today."

3. "Restrictive smoking laws and regulations have sprouted up across the country for all sorts of places, from airplanes and jury rooms to restaurants and office buildings."

4. "The debate ought not be clouded with tobacco industry tactics designed to strip local governments of their basic ability to protect their citizens."

5. "As a result, I believe every New Yorker will live a longer, healthier life."

Faulty Argumentation

A third technique writers commonly use to persuade their readers is the intentional use of faulty reasoning. Formal logic is a branch of philosophy that establishes firm rules for determining whether or not an argument is valid and acceptable. Any violation of these rules is known as a logical fallacy. Because the science of logic is so precise, there are many formally identified violations of these rules. Our purpose here is not to describe and name all of them, but rather to make you aware of some of those commonly used in persuasive writing so that you can better judge the validity of what you are reading. Following are some examples of logical fallacies taken from the readings.

1. "Common courtesy *should* prevail. Do we really need policemen checking smoking compliance in restaurants, on airplanes, in our office buildings?" In this type of fallacy, the assumption is that because one event has occurred, the second will inevitably happen. The writer is suggesting that having smoking laws will automatically cause the police to be present in a place of business to enforce them all the time.

2. "It is time for our elected representatives to rebuff the cigarette lobby and approve a comprehensive statewide smoking control law. . . . " Here, the people who support a position are personally attacked. Instead of giving valid reasons for passing the law, the writer says it should be passed to "rebuff the cigarette lobby."

3. "Need the freedoms of many be abridged by law to relieve the few of occasional minor annoyances?" This faulty reasoning presents the reader with the choice between only two solutions to a problem when, in fact, there are more than two possibilities. The implication here is that the only alternative to having smoking laws would be to limit the freedoms of many people. Notice that this example also uses word choice as a technique to convince the reader.

4. "Most businesses will see to the mutual comfort of smoking or nonsmoking patrons should they perceive the need." In this faulty argument, a conclusion is made based on little or no evidence. Certainly, some businesses may be concerned about the comfort of all their customers, but many others may not be.

5. " . . . overwhelming scientific and medical evidence has conclusively shown the disastrous and tragic effects of tobacco smoking in America. We applaud the governor for his commitment for tight smoking restrictions protecting nonsmokers from involuntary exposure to tobacco smoke. . . . " The faulty logic here is that a comparison is made between two situations that are not similar. While it is true that such evidence exists concerning the effects of smoking on the smoker, there has not been "overwhelming" evidence that ETS has "disastrous and tragic effects" on people who do not smoke. The writer has made an inconsistent comparison.

6. "Smoking restrictions can cause significant financial damage. In Beverly Hills, a strict restaurant smoking ban was repealed after causing a 10 to 30 percent drop in business and millions of dollars in lost revenue." This faulty reasoning makes the assumption that, because one event happened before a second event, the first one is the cause of the second. The false assumption is that the smoking laws caused the loss in revenue, whereas many other factors may have been responsible. It is further assumed that the ban was repealed because of this revenue loss. It is possible that there were other reasons for the repeal of the law, such as complaints from customers.

Practice 4

In the following quotes, try to identify the logical fallacies described above. Do some of them also make use of word choice as a persuasive technique?

1. "The debate ought not be clouded with tobacco industry tactics designed to strip local governments of their basic ability to protect their citizens."

2. " . . . some businessmen believe such laws could put them out of business. As a Santa Monica restauranteur put it, 'If they came in and told me I could allow smoking in [only] one section, and nonsmoking in another . . . I couldn't operate.'"

3. " . . . nuisance laws are 'inflicted' by single-minded persons who look to government to solve personal differences. . . . "

4. "*USA Today* wrote that 'the emerging conflict [over smoking laws] creates a serious hazard in the workplace, turning worker against worker."

   As you can see, it is not always easy to make educated judgments about the articles you read. When writers want to persuade their readers, they can use a number of techniques, sometimes in combination. This is not necessarily a bad thing, but it does become the reader's responsibility to determine whether or not to accept the position presented.

Practice 5

Read the following quotes taken from a variety of articles on the issue of smoking laws. In small groups, try to decide: (a) whether each is fact or opinion, (b) whether any contain words which appeal to the emotions, and (c) whether any contain logical fallacies we have discussed. Remember, a writer may use more than one persuasive technique at a time.

1. "In recent decades, the U.S. tobacco manufacturers have spent untold billions of dollars to protect and expand the sales of their addictive and deadly products."

2. "What legal right, if any, do individuals have to smoke in public places and the workplace? May employers legally give preference to nonsmokers in hiring decisions? The answer to these two questions is clear: The U.S. constitution and federal and state law in general do not recognize, as a legally protected right, the right to smoke."

3. "They're trying to impose their will on everyone—by law. They would build walls, force a new identity on each of us."

4. "Must this new erosion of age-old personal liberties be permitted when the solution is so obvious?"

5. "Individuals are trying, and succeeding, to work out their differences as human beings rather than as smoker and nonsmoker. Another antismoker, after asking 'hundreds' of people to extinguish their cigarettes, cites only one instance when the smoker refused."

6. "Since claims about nonsmoker health are unproven, the question becomes whether it is the business of government to restrict individual freedoms of some that may annoy others."

7. "Enactment of such legislation would lead to more effective enforcement of already existing laws designed to prevent minors' access to a deadly product. It would also shield the public from the insidious practices of the tobacco industry."

8. "Smoking regulations change your image from host . . . to enforcer." (from a brochure written for restaurant owners)

9. "At a time when government is being asked to remove itself from people's lives, laws that attempt to regulate individual choice may create more problems than they solve. Prohibition, the Great Experiment in social reform, had that effect."

10. "These unconscionable peddlers of destruction pose an enormous and well-financed challenge to voluntary health agencies."

11. "Smoking laws place coercive powers of government behind only one side of our hypothetical wall. The likely result? What a Texas newspaper worried could only be 'a decline in good manners.'"

12. "The continued focus on unfounded claims that tobacco smoke compromises the health of nonsmokers will only intensify the current climate of emotionalism and impede the progress of scientific inquiry."

Practice 6

Find and read an article that takes a position on a controversial topic. In the Response section of your Reading Report, point out examples of the three types of persuasive techniques discussed in this chapter.

Topics for Further Investigation

1. Should employers be permitted to require drug testing for their employees?

2. Should marijuana be legalized?

3. Should there be a law requiring the notification of parents of unmarried girls under 18 who want to have an abortion?

4. Are the results of standardized tests, such as the TOEFL, good indicators of a student's abilities, or are they biased?

5. Should the United States have an open immigration policy?

What is the best way to solve the drug problem? An excerpt from a U.S. Government report on pages 111 to 113 offers some suggestions.

Debating an Issue

In Lesson 4, Part B, we talked about class discussions of controversial issues such as abortion, and we emphasized the need for courteous consideration of the opinions of other students. We also talked about the role of the group leader in directing such a discussion, making sure that the opinions of all members of the group were expressed. In this lesson, we will examine another way to talk about a controversial issue: a debate.

What Is a Debate?

A debate is, according to the dictionary, "a contest in which the affirmative and negative sides of a proposition are advocated by opposing speakers." That is, a debate is a contest to see which side, or team, presents its opinions in the best way. The proposition is a statement on a controversial issue, and each team argues either *for* or *against* it.

The proposition might be a statement such as, "All abortions should be against the law." One team would argue *for* the proposition, agreeing that all abortions should be against the law, perhaps focusing on abortion as murder, and arguing for the rights of the unborn child. The other team would argue *against* the proposition, probably focusing on the problems of rape, incest, the possibility of a deformed fetus, and the rights of the mother.

Since a debate is a contest, there are rules which are agreed to before the debate begins. These rules govern the amount of time each team has to present its position, the amount of time for questions, and the amount of time for concluding statements. The moderator, a neutral person such as the teacher or a student who is not a member of either team, is responsible for seeing that the two teams stick to the time allowed them for each part of the debate.

The participants may also agree to criteria for judging the quality of their arguments and at the end of the debate, points may be awarded to each team and a winner declared. Debates may be formal or informal. The study of formal debating is called "forensics." During formal debates, strict rules are followed and professional judges award points and decide which team has won. In this class, you will participate in an informal debate.

The topic of drug abuse, drug trafficking, and law enforcement is a controversial one, and one that could lend itself to a debate of a number of interesting issues. In this lesson, you are going to read an article about drug abuse in the United States and what the government proposes to do about stopping it. The article is excerpted from the introduction to the 1990 presidential report entitled *National Drug Enforcement Strategy*, written by William J. Bennett, Director of the Office of National Drug Control Policy. As you read the article, think of topics that might be proposed for a debate. Also consider this question, "Is the purpose of the writer to inform or to convince?" Look for language cues: is the tone neutral, or are there words and phrases which carry an emotional message? Use techniques you learned in Lesson 1, Part C, to help you make your judgments.

SPECIALIZED VOCABULARY

1. homicide—the killing of one human being by another
2. felony—a serious crime punishable by a year or more in prison
3. robbery—stealing something from a person by force
4. burglary—breaking into a home or business to steal
5. assault—an attack on one person by another
6. drug trafficking—the smuggling or secret transport, buying, and selling of drugs
7. black market—the illegal buying and selling of goods
8. drug cartel—an international group of criminals who try to control the prices and distribution of illegal drugs
9. insurgencies—attempts to overthrow the legal government by force
10. addict—a person who cannot do without drugs
11. interdiction—finding illegal drugs and preventing them from entering the country
12. habit—having to take drugs, a drug addiction
13. paranoia—a type of mental illness in which people have an unreasonable fear and suspicion of others

Introduction

In late July of this year, the Federal government's National Institute on Drug Abuse (NIDA) released the results of its ninth periodic National Household Survey on Drug Abuse—the first such comprehensive, national study of drug use patterns since 1985. Much of the news in NIDA's report was dramatic and startling. The estimated number of Americans using *any* illegal drug on a "current" basis (in other words, at least once in the 30-day period preceding the survey) has dropped 37 percent: from 23 million in 1985 to 14.5 million last year. Current use of the two most common illegal substances—marijuana and cocaine—is down 36 and 48 percent respectively.

This is all good news—very good news. But it is also, at first glance, difficult to square with commonsense perceptions. Most Americans remain firmly convinced that drugs represent the gravest present threat to our national well-being—and with good reason. Because a wealth of other, up-to-date evidence suggests that our drug problem is getting worse, not better.

Crime.   Fear of drugs and attendant crime are at an all-time high. Rates of drug-related homicide continue to rise—sometimes alarmingly—in cities across the country. Felony drug convictions now account for the single largest and fastest growing sector of the Federal prison population. Three-fourths of all robberies and half of all felony assaults committed by young people (statistically, the most crime-prone age group) now involve drug users. Reports of bystander deaths due to drug-related gunfights and drive-by shootings continue to climb.

Health.   The threat drugs pose to American public health has never been greater. Intravenous drug use is now the single largest source of new HIV/AIDS virus infections, and perhaps one-half of all AIDS deaths are drug-related. The number of drug-related emergency hospital admissions increased by 121 percent between 1985 and 1988. As many as 200,000 babies are born each year to mothers who use drugs. Many of these infants suffer low birth weight, severe and often permanent mental and physical dysfunction or impairment, or signs of actual drug dependence. Many other such babies—born many weeks or months premature—do not survive past infancy.

The Economy.   Drug trafficking, distribution, and sales in America have become a vast, economically debilitating black market. One U.S. Chamber of Commerce estimate puts annual gross drug sales at $110 billion—more than our total gross agricultural income, and more than double the profits enjoyed by all the *Fortune* 500 companies combined. Such figures cannot truly be calculated with any real precision, but it is all too clear that drug use acts as a direct and painful brake on American competitiveness. One study reports that on-the-job drug use alone costs American industry and business $60 billion a year in lost productivity and drug-related accidents.

Overseas.   In Southeast and West Asia, South and Central America, and the Caribbean Basin, drug exporting networks and domestic drug use are causing serious social, economic, and political disruptions. Intense drug-inspired violence or official corruption have plagued a number of Latin American countries for years; in more than one of them, drug cartel operations and associated local insurgencies are a real and present danger to democratic institutions, national economies, and basic civil order. In Pakistan, the number of heroin addicts has more than tripled in the past four years alone. And so, because our national security directly depends on regional stability throughout the Americas and across the globe, drugs have become a major concern of U.S. foreign policy.   (*continued*)

Availability. Finally, undeniably, the fact remains that here in the United States, in every State—in our cities, in our suburbs, in our rural communities—drugs are potent, drugs are cheap, and drugs are available to almost anyone who wants them.

Thinking About Drugs and Public Policy

What, generally speaking, should we do? What's the best way to fight drugs and drug use? It is a broad and complicated question. It is also a question the United States has struggled with inconclusively for many decades.

Facing understandable public outrage and alarm over the terrible consequences of widespread drug use, Federal, State, and local governments have repeatedly sought to concentrate dramatic responsive action against one or another point on the drug-problem continuum: first through law enforcement; later through a combination of education and treatment efforts; and most recently through heavy emphasis on interdiction of imported drugs at our borders.

Most Americans correctly view drugs as a personal tragedy for those who use them. Most Americans are eager to provide drug users with the medical attention that can help them stop, and young people with the social and educational training that can help prevent them from starting in the first place. Neither goal is a primary concern of law enforcement. So does it then follow that we should undertake a massive shift of emphasis away from drug enforcement and toward, instead, treatment for addicts and counseling for students?

Some people think so. Consider the argument in its starkest and most extreme form. Hardly a week goes by these days in which some serious forum or other—a national news magazine, for example, or the opinion page of a major newspaper, or a scholarly conference or television panel discussion—fails to give solemn consideration to the advocacy of wholesale drug legalization. Legalization's proponents generally say something like this: Enforcing our many laws against drugs is a terribly expensive and difficult business. Were we to repeal those laws, drug-related crime would vanish, and the time and money saved in reduced law enforcement could be more effectively spent on health care for addicts and on preventive instruction for the rest of us.

Exactly how under this scenario we could convincingly warn potential new users about the evils of drugs—having just made them legally acceptable—is not entirely clear. Nor is it clear how an already overburdened treatment system could possibly respond to what candid legalization proponents themselves admit would probably be a sharply increased rate of overall drug use. The cost of drugs—measured in purchase price, the time it takes to search them out, and the risks involved due to unreliable ''quality'' and legal sanction—is a key predictor of drug use. Cheaper, easier-to-get, and ''better'' legalized drugs would likely mean more drug users and more frequent drug use.

And would legalization actually reduce crime? Crimes committed by addicts to pay for their habits might theoretically decline a bit. But since addicts use drugs—especially cocaine—as often as they can, less expensive drugs might just as well mean more frequent purchases and a still-constant need for cash-producing burglaries and robberies. What's more, since cocaine use is known to produce dangerous behavioral side-effects—paranoia, irritability, and quick resort to violence on minimal provocation—legalization might also entail an increase in more serious crime by addicts.

Drug traffickers, by contrast, are involved in crime for profit alone. An average gram of cocaine now sells for $60 to $80. The free-market price would be roughly 5 percent of that—$3 or $4. If legalized drug sales were heavily regulated and taxed to restrict availability and maximize government revenue, then a gram of cocaine might sell for $30 or $40. In that case, criminal organizations could still undercut legal prices and turn a substantial profit. In truth, to destroy the cocaine black market entirely, we would probably have to make the drug legally available at not much more than $10 a gram. And then an average dose of cocaine would cost about 50 cents—well within the lunch-money budget of the average American elementary school student.

In short, legalizing drugs would be an unqualified national disaster. In fact, *any* significant relaxation of drug enforcement — for whatever reason, however well-intentioned— would promise more use, more crime, and more trouble for desperately needed treatment and education efforts.

The United States has a broad array of tools at its disposal, in government and out, each of which—in proper combination with the others—can and does have a significant effect on the shape and size of our drug problem. We must use them all. We must have what we have never had before: a comprehensive, fully integrated national drug control strategy. It must proceed from a proper understanding of all that we do and do not know about drugs. It must take calm and intelligent measure of the strengths and limitations of specific available drug control initiatives. And it must then begin to intensify and calibrate them so that the number of Americans who still use cocaine and other illegal drugs, to the entire nation's horrible disadvantage, is—more and more as time goes by—dramatically reduced.

Reprinted from William J. Bennett, "Introduction," *National Drug Control Strategy*, 5 September 1989, 1–14.

Questions for Discussion

1. Which is more important and more effective in combating drug abuse, limiting the *supply* of drugs, or the *demand* for them? Why?

2. Should any drugs be legalized? marijuana? cocaine? heroin? Why, or why not?

3. What is the current drug situation in your country? What is the law? What is the reality?

4. What is the role of organized crime in drug trafficking? What happens on the local level? What happens on the international level?

5. How is drug abuse really a world problem? What should the nations of the world community do to deal with it? What are the priorities?

6. What is the purpose of this article? Is it neutral, or does the author take a stand?

Practice 1

The following sentences contain key words and phrases from the reading. Paraphrase the parts indicated to show that you understand their meaning. Try to do this practice without using a dictionary.

1. "Current use of the two most common *illegal **substances**—mari-juana and cocaine—is down 36 and 48 percent respectively."

2. "*Felony drug **convictions*** now account for the single largest and fastest growing sector of the Federal prison population."

3. "*The threat drugs **pose*** to American public health has never been greater."

4. "Many other such babies—born many weeks or months prema-ture—*do not **survive** past infancy*."

5. "And so, because our national security directly depends on regional stability throughout the Americas and across the globe, drugs *have become a **major concern*** of U.S. foreign policy."

6. "Hardly a week goes by these days in which *some serious **forum** or other*—a national news magazine, for example, or the opinion page of a major newspaper, or a scholarly conference or televi-sion panel discussion—fails to give solemn consideration to the advocacy of wholesale drug legalization."

7. "*Legalization's **proponents*** generally say something like this: Enforcing our many laws against drugs is a terribly expensive and difficult business."

8. "And would legalization actually reduce crime? Crimes commit-ted by addicts to pay for their habits might theoretically ***decline a bit***."

9. "What's more, since cocaine use is known to produce dangerous behavioral ***side-effects**—paranoia, irritability, and quick resort to violence on minimal provocation—legalization might also entail an increase in more serious crime by addicts."

10. "We must have what we never had before: a comprehensive, fully integrated national drug control strategy. *It must **proceed from*** a proper understanding of all that we do and do not know about drugs."

Check Your Progress

Look at the following useful words from the reading. If there are any you don't recognize or know how to use, consider adding them to your vocabulary list.

comprehensive	productivity	potent
current	disruption	continuum
competitiveness	export	array
stability	corruption	strategy

Gathering Information for a Debate

The drug problem raises many issues that could be debated. One of these issues is whether legalizing drugs would really help to eliminate them. A proposition to debate might be "All drugs should be legalized and regulated by the government." If you were on the team arguing *for* this proposition, you would find reasons why legalizing drugs would help end drug-related crime, and enable the government to use its resources to control drugs and ultimately stop their abuse. If you were arguing *against* this proposition, you would present all the reasons why legalizing drugs would increase their usage and actually make the problem much worse.

To find reasons for or against legalizing drugs, it would be necessary to do research. You would have to locate books or articles which would provide facts you could use in your debate. You would have to analyze the articles, using techniques suggested in Lesson 1, Part C, to separate fact from opinion. You would evaluate the quality of the evidence the author presented to support an argument for or against legalizing drugs. It would be important to recognize whether the author's purpose was to *inform* or to *convince* when you made these judgments.

The purpose of the article you just read is to inform the United States Congress and the general public about the current state of the drug problem and to make recommendations about how to solve it. The president, as chief executive of the executive branch of the government, has been required to have his Office of Drug Control Policy prepare this report and submit it to Congress each year since 1988. The first purpose of the report is to provide information, but the tone of the report is not completely neutral, is it? This is because the writer wishes to convince Congress and the general public to accept the recommendations that he is making.

Look at, for example, the section in which Bennett discusses whether or not drugs should be legalized. He concludes, "In short, legalizing drugs would be an unqualified disaster." The word *disaster* is quite strong, but Bennett makes his statement even more forceful by adding the word *unqualified*. Bennett insists that the government should *not* legalize drugs. In order to persuade us that he has considered both sides of the issue and that we should accept this recommendation, he presents his arguments in the form of a mini-debate. Beginning in the middle of the fifth paragraph on page 112, he states the reasons that have been given for legalizing drugs, and then he explains why this approach will not work.

Even the language Bennett uses to present the arguments *for* legalizing drugs is slanted because of his word choice. He states that proponents for legalization argue that "Enforcing our many laws against drugs is a terribly expensive and difficult business. Were we to repeal those laws, drug-related crime would vanish, and the time and money saved in reduced law enforcement could be more effectively spent on health care for addicts, and on preventive instruction for the rest of us." To paraphrase, Bennett says that the arguments presented by the proponents of legalizing drugs are:

1. There are many laws that have to be enforced.
2. Enforcing the laws is "terribly expensive."
3. Enforcing the laws is very "difficult."
4. If we repealed the laws, drug-related crime would "vanish."
5. We could save a lot of time and money.
6. This time and money could then be spent on health care for addicts.
7. It could also be spent on preventing drug abuse through education programs.

In the first sentence, Bennett implies that those who advocate legalizing drugs probably believe that enforcing the laws is a pretty impossible task, and the money would be better spent another way. In the next sentence, Bennett implies that proponents of legalizing drugs claim that legalization would cause drug-related crime to disappear completely. Here, his use of the word *vanish* is very strong.

Practice 2

Read through the rest of this section, and list the arguments Bennett uses to persuade us that legalizing drugs would be a terrible mistake. Use the following questions as a guide.

1. What problem of logic might those who are conducting drug prevention programs face?
2. What would probably happen to the overall rate of drug use? Do the proponents of legalization acknowledge that?
3. What three risks now discourage people from using drugs? What effect would legalizing drugs have on these risks? What would be the expected result?
4. What are two reasons why there might *not* be a decline in the number of crimes committed by drug addicts?
5. If the government were selling legalized drugs at half the cost they are now sold on the street, how could organized crime continue to make a profit by selling drugs illegally?
6. At what price would the government have to sell a gram of cocaine to make it unprofitable for organized crime to continue selling drugs on the black market? What problem would such a low price cause?

If you were preparing to argue in favor of the proposition "Drugs Should Not Be Legalized," this article would provide some very useful information. Some of the information is factual, and because this is a government document, it is a credible source. Some of the information is in the form of conclusions drawn from looking at the evidence, and it constitutes the recommendations the government is proposing. The article would also be useful because it presents the pros and cons of legalization in the form of a mini-debate to help you anticipate what the other side might say.

Finally, the author of the article uses language and strategies that you might want to incorporate into your presentation if you were arguing *against* legalization. For example, consider the emotional impact of this statement: "And then an average dose of cocaine would cost about 50 cents—well within the lunch-money budget of the average American elementary school student." This is an excellent scare tactic; imagine cocaine being so cheap that little children could afford to buy it by using their lunch money!

Practice 3

Read the following excerpt from the article and decide what impact the highlighted words and phrases have. Why did the author choose these words? Which emotion he is appealing to?

> And would legalization **actually** reduce crime? Crimes committed by addicts to pay for their habits might **theoretically** decline **a bit**. But since **addicts use drugs—especially cocaine—as often as they can**, less expensive drugs might just as well mean **more frequent purchases** and a **still-constant need** for cash-producing **burglaries** and **robberies**. What's more, since cocaine use is known to produce **dangerous behavioral side-effects—paranoia, irritability**, and **quick resort to violence** on **minimal provocation**—legalization might also entail an **increase in more serious crime** by addicts.

The Format of an Informal Debate

1. **Introductory Statements:** Each team introduces the arguments for its side. The "pro" team presents the arguments in favor of the proposition, and the "con" team presents the arguments against it. The team leader may present the remarks, or the various points may be divided up among members of the team, giving each team member a chance to speak.

2. **Questions:** After each team has made its opening statements, the other team has a chance to ask questions. All members of the opposing teams may ask or answer questions. The goal of the questioners is to discredit the position of the other team. Those answering questions will attempt to defend their position.

3. **Concluding Statements:** After the question period is over, there should be a break of five minutes to allow the teams a chance to prepare their concluding remarks. Each team leader then makes a concluding statement, summarizing the team's strongest arguments and pointing out weaknesses in the arguments of the opposing team. The class may then award points for each group or vote to determine which team wins the debate.

Planning for a Debate

1. Decide on a proposition to be debated. Remember that it must be a statement that one side can argue in favor of and the other side can argue against.

2. Choose two teams to argue the opposing sides of the proposition. It is a good idea to limit the number of team members to three or four per team, so that each member of the team has a chance to speak.

3. Decide on the amount of time that will be allowed for each part of the debate: the introductory statements, the questions, and the concluding statements. Decide whether the introductory remarks will be made by the team leader or by all the team members. If the team members speak, how much time should each one have? (If the debate is to be done within a class hour, you may wish to allow 10 or 15 minutes for each part of the debate. Then, each team member could make an introductory statement of three minutes, for example.)

4. Decide who will moderate the debate.

5. Decide if the teams will be judged by the other members of the class. Will a winner be chosen? Will points be awarded? Will a vote be taken?

Preparing for the Debate

1. Each team chooses a leader and a reporter.

2. The leader conducts a discussion of possible arguments to be used in the debate. The reporter writes the ideas on a Group Discussion Report Form.

3. The group determines what research needs to be done on the topic and how to go about it. Who will do what? This information is also recorded on the Group Discussion Report Form.

4. After the research is completed, each team prepares its arguments. The reporter writes down the points to be presented, and the group decides who will present which point.

5. The team anticipates questions the other team might ask and then decides what response they could make to each question.

6. The group lists questions they want to ask the opposing team and decides who should ask what question.

7. The team lists its strongest arguments and prepares the concluding statement. (This will be revised during the five-minute break during the debate, just before the teams deliver their closing remarks.)

Conducting the Debate

1. The two teams sit facing each other with the moderator between them. The moderator uses a stopwatch or other timing device to keep track of the time. (A suggested timeframe is given for each part.) The moderator makes sure that the teams stay within their allotted times and that everyone speaks courteously and respectfully.

2. The "pro" team presents its introductory statements. (8–10 min.)

3. The "con" team asks them questions, and each question is answered one at a time. Any member of the "pro" team may answer a question. (8–10 min.)

4. The "con" team presents its introductory statements. (8–10 min.)

5. The "pro" team asks them questions and the "con" team members answer them. (8–10 min.)

6. There is a five-minute break so that the teams may prepare their concluding statements. (5 min.)

7. The "con" team presents its concluding statement. (3–5 min.)

8. The "pro" team presents its concluding statement. (3–5 min.)

9. The class rates the teams and votes for the winner.

Evaluating the Debate

Practice 4

Plan, prepare for, and conduct a class debate following the directions given. You may choose to debate the question of legalizing drugs or another drug-related topic, or you may choose something else. Here are some suggestions for rating the performance of each team.

1. How convincing were the arguments presented?

2. Were the arguments supported with facts or examples?

3. Were the introductory statements clear and well organized?

4. Did the questions address weaknesses in the opposing team's position?

5. How well did the team respond to the opposing team's questions?

6. Were the concluding statements clear and well organized?

7. Did all the members of the team participate?

8. Did the team members look and act forceful and confident?

Topics for Further Research

1. The drug policies of the United Nations

2. The drug cartels of the Latin American countries

3. Options for drug treatment

4. How the United States may use foreign policy to fight drug trafficking

Is there anything we can do about global warming? Read the articles about the greenhouse effect on pages 122 to 130 to get an overview.

Synthesizing Information

In this lesson, we will focus on a skill that readers regularly use when they are particularly interested in one aspect of a general subject: synthesis. To synthesize means to draw information on the same topic from several sources and then to integrate it into a new form. In other words, you will be reading several texts on the same topic in order to find information about one particular aspect of the topic.

Initially, this may seem to be an overwhelming task, particularly when you are dealing with a complex issue. However, if this type of reading is approached systematically, it can become an interesting challenge rather than a chore. This chapter will show you how, using the same techniques you have been practicing, to synthesize efficiently from your reading.

Unlike previous lessons, this one contains three articles excerpted from an issue of the *EPA Journal*, a publication of the U.S. government's Environmental Protection Agency. All three articles focus on the serious problem of global warming, known as the Greenhouse Effect. Each deals with a different aspect of the problem, but they all contain certain specific information on some of the same issues.

Common to many forms of academic writing, these articles are preceded by an abstract, a brief overview of the issues discussed in the article. Academic writers frequently provide an abstract so that readers can determine whether the article will be of help or interest to them.

SPECIALIZED VOCABULARY FOR READING 1

1. carbon dioxide (CO_2)—a colorless, odorless gas which passes out of the blood in breathing
2. trace gases—an amount of gas so small that it is barely perceptible
3. Ice Age—a period when much of the earth was covered with ice
4. glacial melting—the gradual changing of glacial ice into water
5. fossil fuel—fuel dug from the earth, as in coal
6. deforestation—the clearing of forests and woodlands

Reading 1: "A Character Sketch of Greenhouse"

ABSTRACT This article describes what is meant by the "Greenhouse Effect" and distinguishes between what scientists really know about it and what is merely speculation. There is also discussion of the seriousness of the predictions about the coming global warming trend. The author concludes by making suggestions on how we might slow down the warming process.

A Character Sketch of Greenhouse   by Dr. David Rind

The Greenhouse Effect has caught the imagination of the general populace in the last decade. What's more, the respected, generally conservative scientific establishment has become associated with relatively dire predictions of future climate changes the Greenhouse Effect may cause.

But how much do we actually know about the Greenhouse Effect? Can we really establish how much the climate will change, and when? Perhaps by separating the "hard" science—that which can be verified and is considered well-understood—from scientific theory or estimates, we *can* investigate the likelihood of near-term climate changes that have been projected. The series of questions which follow will help us explore what we currently know, or think we know, about the Greenhouse Effect.

Question: Do we really understand the "Greenhouse Effect"?

The "Greenhouse Effect" is the name for the physical process whereby energy from the sun passes through the atmosphere relatively freely, while heat radiating from the earth is partially blocked or absorbed by particular gases in the atmosphere. Because the sun is warmer than the earth, its energy is radiated at a higher frequency which is not absorbed well by gases such as carbon dioxide (CO_2) or water vapor. In contrast, these triatomic gases (gases with three atoms per molecule) are effective absorbers of the lower-frequency energy radiated by the earth. Since the gases responsible for this selective absorption make up only about one percent of the atmosphere, they are known as "trace" gases. In general, we can calculate very accurately the energy absorbed by different gases, although there are some uncertainties, and when the concentration of a gas changes, we know how much more energy is being absorbed. This additional absorption by itself warms the planet: for example, doubling the concentration of CO_2 in the atmosphere would eventually lead to a global air temperature increase of 1.2° Centigrade (C)—about 2.2° Fahrenheit (F)—if there were no other changes in the climate system.

However, what we do *not* know is exactly how the rest of the system will react. The current numerical computer models of the earth's climate predict that the warming due to the increase in CO_2 will lead to more evaporation of water vapor from the ocean. Water vapor itself is a "greenhouse" gas, so as its concentration increases in the atmosphere, the planet will warm even further. With rising temperatures there will be less snow and ice to reflect energy from the sun back to space (snow and ice are very good reflectors). This promotes further warming because more of the sun's heat is retained in the earth.

These are examples of "positive feedbacks" in which the system responds to a warming climate with changes which amplify the warming even further. Both of these system responses are very likely to occur, although we cannot be sure of the magnitude of the changes. The models also predict cloud cover changes that will provide even more warming, but clouds are not modeled in a very sophisticated way because they are not well understood. Thus, the likely impact of cloud cover changes is quite uncertain.

The net result of these different processes in the various models is the tripling of the warming caused by the doubled CO_2 levels alone, producing a total warming of about 4°C (or 7°F) for the global, annual average. Yet it is only the initial Greenhouse Effect due to increased CO_2 or increases in other trace gases, which we know with great confidence.

Question: How "dire" is the forecast of coming climate change?

It is estimated that the ice age climate was some 4°C colder than today's. At that time (some 18,000 years ago), ice covered the area now occupied by New York City. Considering that the doubled CO_2 climate is estimated to be warmer to the same degree that the ice ages were cooler, large changes in the climate system may well be expected if this comes to pass. The GISS model's forecast for the next 50 years gives changes of 2°C (3.6°F) by the year 2020, which would make the earth warmer than it is thought to have been at any point in historical time. Estimates for summer temperatures in the doubled CO_2 climate indicate that Washington, DC, which currently experiences 36 days of temperature above 90°F would routinely have 87 such days; Dallas would go from 19 days with temperatures above 100°F to 78 days.

Sea-level rise due to thermal expansion of the oceans would cause severe problems in many coastal cities, and this effect would be exacerbated if additional glacial melting occurred. Rainfall patterns would likely be substantially altered, posing the threat of large-scale disruptions of agricultural and economic productivity, and water shortages in some areas.

We may start experiencing the effects of a changing climate fairly soon. If we define a "hot" summer as the warmest one-third of the summers during the period 1950–1980, then, if the models are correct, during the 1990s we will experience "hot" summers twice as often, or two-thirds of the time. The summer of 1988 may be an all-too-tangible indication of how dire such changes in summertime climate can be.

Question: Is there any way to prevent these changes from occurring?

The climate is being altered by the release of greenhouse gases due to fossil fuel consumption and industrial processes, and by deforestation. These factors are inherent in our current civilization. It may be possible to limit specific trace gas increases (such as the CFCs) and slow down rates of increase of CO_2 through increased energy conservation. Our ability to manipulate the climate system deliberately, so as to offset the warming by some other process, is nonexistent. It is likely that the additional greenhouse gases which have been added to the atmosphere during the past 50 years have already built considerable warming into the system, which we have not yet experienced because of the slow warming response of the ocean.

The climate of the next century will very likely be substantially different from that to which we have become accustomed. Uncertainties in our knowledge of the true climate sensitivity prevent us from knowing exactly how different it will be. The consequences of the climate change that is currently being estimated would be enormous. With that in mind, it is worthwhile for us to factor climatic change into decision-making processes related to our future, even though there are many uncertainties that still exist in our understanding of what may actually happen.

(Dr. Rind is an atmospheric scientist at the Institute for Space Studies, Goddard Space Flight Center, National Aeronautics and Space Administration, and an adjunct associate professor at Columbia University. He is a leading researcher on aspects of the greenhouse theory of atmospheric warming from certain gases.)

Reprinted from David Rind, "A Character Sketch of Greenhouse," *EPA Journal*, January 1989, 4.

Manmade Contributions to the
Greenhouse Effect

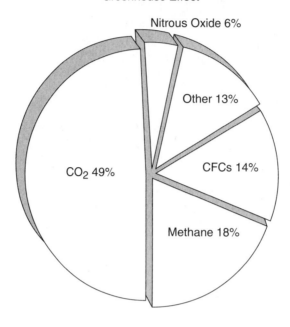

Regional Contributions to the
Greenhouse Effect

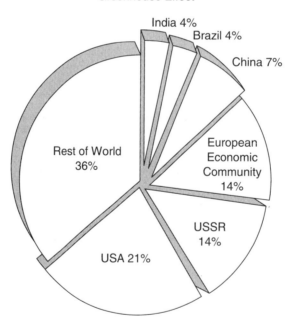

(The top chart represents the estimated increase in the Greenhouse
Effect due to manmade emissions of Greenhouse gases in the 1980s.
The chart is adapted from work by Dr. James Hansen and his associates
at the Goddard Institute for Space Studies. The bottom chart is based
on EPA estimates of each region's contribution to manmade emissions
of Greenhouse gases.)

SPECIALIZED VOCABULARY FOR READING 2

1. oxidize—to unite chemically with oxygen (as in burning or rusting)
2. respiration—the act or process of breathing
3. photosynthesis—production of organic substances from carbon dioxide and water by the action of sunlight on the chlorophyll in green plants
4. ecologists—scientists who study the relationship between living things and their environment
5. nutrient—anything that nourishes; food
6. ecosystem—a community of animals and plants interrelated with their environment

Reading 2: "Part of the Problem and Part of the Answer"

ABSTRACT   This article stresses the important role that forests and woodlands may play in both hastening and slowing the Greenhouse Effect. Deforestation has contributed to the earth's warming by eliminating a source for CO_2 through photosynthesis, yet new trees may grow faster as a result of this warming. Although no one can be certain of the effects of forests on the environment, the author feels that protecting those still in existence and replanting those that have already been destroyed should be an international priority.

Part of the Problem and Part of the Answer   by Sandra Postel

Over the last century—a mere instant of geologic time—the activities of the human species have caused unprecedented changes in the atmosphere. A continuing buildup of certain chemical compounds—most importantly, carbon dioxide (CO_2)—is propelling the environment towards [a] potentially catastrophic shift. . . . Fossil fuel combustion has spewed 150 to 190 billion tons of carbon into the air, and forest clearing for cropland and fuelwood has contributed an additional 90 to 180 billion tons. . . .

While some climatic change is inevitable, societies can gain precious time to adapt if action is taken now to dampen its ultimate magnitude and slow its pace. The first step requires curbing the use of fossil fuels, now the leading cause of the CO_2 buildup.

But there is another step crucial to restoring atmospheric balance: protecting our remaining forests and planting more trees. Forests and woodlands are vast storehouses of carbon, so clearing and burning them—as is now happening on a large scale in the tropics—contributes to CO_2-induced climate change. Because trees remove CO_2 from the air through photosynthesis, planting more of them can be part of the remedy. Therein lies an opportunity to capitalize on the enduring link between earthly life and the atmosphere—by reforesting the earth. . . .

The earth's trees, shrubs, and soils hold about two trillion tons of carbon, roughly triple the amount stored in the atmosphere. When vegetation is cleared and burned, or just left to decay, the carbon it contains, along with some of that in the underlying soil, is oxidized and released to join the atmospheric pool of CO_2.

Today the bulk of the CO_2 emitted from the land in this way comes from developing countries in the tropics. Each year, 28 million acres of tropical forest are destroyed through the combined action of land clearing for crop production, fuelwood gathering, and cattle ranching. Commercial timber harvesting degrades an additional 11 million acres. All told, an area of trees slightly larger than New York and Vermont combined is lost or logged each year.

> **There is another step crucial to restoring atmospheric balance: protecting our remaining forests and planting more trees.**

A worrisome twist to the forest/climate change link is how the world's remaining forests will behave in a warmer climate and an atmosphere richer in CO_2. . . .

Higher CO_2 levels usually have a fertilizing effect on plants, spurring them to grow faster. . . . If trees did indeed grow faster as atmospheric CO_2 levels increased, they would remove carbon from the atmosphere more rapidly. This "negative feedback" would help slow the global warming. So far, unfortunately, no convincing evidence suggests that trees in their natural environments would respond this way. . . .

Another possibility results in positive feedback, a worsening of the warming trend. George Woodwell, director of the Woods Hole Research Institute, points out that as temperatures rise, trees and microorganisms in the soil substantially increase their rates of respiration. . . . The danger is that an increase in respiration because of rising temperatures could release more CO_2 to the atmosphere, reinforcing the very buildup that initiated the warming.

If respiration exceeded photosynthesis for an extended period of time, trees would stop growing altogether and ultimately die. . . . Woodwell maintains that a widespread forest die-off could release enormous amounts of carbon to the atmosphere—perhaps hundreds of billions of tons—depending on the speed of the warming. He warns that "the sudden destruction of forests by air pollution, now being experienced in northern and central Europe . . . is but a sample of the destruction that appears to be in store."

Woodwell's scenario might never come to pass. Ecologists do not yet agree on how forests will respond to a warmer climate, or even on whether that response will add CO_2 to the atmosphere or remove it. Some point out, for example, that higher temperatures would increase rates of organic decomposition, which in turn would release nutrients to the soil and thus potentially boost the productivity of trees. This could cause a helpful negative feedback: since trees would be growing faster, they would remove more CO_2 from the atmosphere, helping slow the warming.

How forests will actually respond looms large in the climate change picture, since the potential for a strong feedback—positive or negative—clearly exists.

Protecting forests and planting trees need to be high on the international agenda for several compelling reasons other than stabilizing the global carbon cycle. The growing wave of deforestation has left in its wake a severe energy crisis in the Third World (wood provides the primary source of energy for more than two-thirds of the people in developing countries), an accelerating loss of the earth's biological diversity, and large areas of degraded land. . . .

Countries are unlikely to invest substantial resources in tree planting solely to ward off global warming. But, in much of the Third World, satisfying fuelwood needs and restoring productivity to degraded ecosystems provide a sound—even urgent—rationale.

A worrisome twist to the forest/climate change link is how the world's remaining forests will behave in a warmer climate and an atmosphere richer in CO_2. . . .

Of course, slowing the destruction of existing forests is also crucial. Halving the CO_2 contribution from deforestation in Brazil, Indonesia, Colombia, and the Ivory Coast would reduce net carbon emissions from tropical forests by more than 20 percent. Together, that achievement and the carbon-storage benefits of 300 million acres of trees would cut releases from tropical forests by two-thirds. The total amount of carbon added to the atmosphere from all human activities—deforestation and fossil fuel combustion—would be cut by 17 percent.

Can the community of nations plant trees on the scale required to improve prospects in the Third World and simultaneously help balance the global carbon cycle? There are reasons for optimism.

International development agencies now recognize that rural people form the only labor force large enough to plant trees on the vast scale that is needed. More than ever before, this labor force is being mobilized into action. . . .

International relief agencies, such as CARE in the United States and Oxfam in the United Kingdom, have orchestrated some of the most successful reforestation projects to date.

Worldwide, thousands of women's groups, peasant collectives, churches and other small, local organizations have taken up the cause of tree planting. . . . Kenya's Greenbelt Movement . . . has enlisted . . . more than 15,000 farmers and a half-million schoolchildren in setting up 670 community nurseries and planting more than two million trees. . . .

Chinese officials have set a goal of getting 20 percent of their country's territory in trees by the year 2000. . . . Indian Prime Minister Rajiv Ghandi tripled funding for forestry in his development agenda for 1985–90, gave forestry new prominence within his ministries, and created a National Wastelands Development Board to spearhead a "people's movement" for reforestation. . . .

Reforestation's potential to help avert climate change barely gets mentioned in reports or plans that sketch out forestry's future. But as the consequences of global warming become clearer, and their magnitude and cost hit home, tree planting solely for the purpose of stabilizing climate could appear on the international agenda.

Reprinted from Sandra Postel, "Part of the Problem and Part of the Answer," *EPA Journal*, January 1989, 44.

SPECIALIZED VOCABULARY FOR READING 3

1. wetlands—swampy areas surrounding rivers, oceans, and lakes

2. salinity—consisting of or containing salt

3. acidity—possessing or containing chemical compounds that react with a base to form salt

4. yellow fever—a tropical disease caused by a virus transmitted by a mosquito bite, characterized by fever, vomiting, and yellowing of the skin

5. malaria—a recurring infectious disease (also transmitted by a mosquito bite) characterized by chills and fever

6. ozone layer—a protective layer of gases surrounding the earth's atmosphere

7. depleting—using up

8. tropospheric—having to do with the atmosphere from the earth's surface to about 6 to 12 miles above

9. stratospheric—having to do with the atmosphere extending beyond the troposphere (beyond 12 to 15 miles)

10. reforestation—the process of planting new trees in forests to replace those which have been cut down

Reading 3: "With a Global Focus"

ABSTRACT   This article focuses on the need for international cooperation in trying to control the Greenhouse Effect by describing the results that global warming would have on us and the way we live. The efforts to control the potential effects of the warming climate by international organizations such as the United Nations are described. The author concludes by calling for more action on both the governmental and individual levels.

With a Global Focus by William H. Mansfield III

"Global warming may be the greatest challenge facing humankind," according to Dr. Mostafa K. Tolba, Executive Director of the United Nations Environmental Programme (UNEP) and Under Secretary General of the United Nations. Indeed, the mounting concern about climate change impacts has sent storm warning flags aloft in the United Nations, where the President of the Maldives, Maumoon Abdul Gayoom, gave a dramatic, impassioned address to the 1987 U.N. General Assembly on the severe consequences of sea-level rise on his low-lying island country. Malta put a resolution on the same issue poignantly before the 1988 General Assembly. The resolution was adopted, and a meeting of heads of U.N. organizations on environmental matters in Paris in July 1988 featured climate change as a major discussion item. It was also a major topic at the Economic Summit in Toronto last June.

Sea-level rise as a consequence of global warming would immediately threaten that large fraction of the globe living at sea level. Nearly one-third of all human beings live within 36 miles of a coastline. Most of the world's great seaport cities would be endangered: New Orleans, Amsterdam, Shanghai, Cairo. Some countries—Maldives Islands in the Indian Ocean, islands in the Pacific—would be inundated. Heavily populated coastal areas such as in Bangladesh and Egypt, where large populations occupy low-lying areas, would suffer extreme dislocation.

Warmer oceans would spawn stronger hurricanes and typhoons, resulting in coastal flooding, possibly swamping valuable agricultural lands around the world. Reduced water quality may result as coastal flooding forces salt water into coastal irrigation and drinking water supplies, and irreplaceable, natural wetlands could be flooded with ocean water, destroying forever many of the unique plant and animal species living there.

Food supplies and forests would be adversely affected. Changes in rainfall patterns would disrupt agriculture. Warmer temperatures would shift grain-growing regions polewards. The warming would also increase and change the pest plants, such as weeds, and the insects attacking the crops.

> The precedent established in tackling the stratospheric ozone issue may well be a useful model for dealing with climate change. But climate change is an infinitely more complex issue to deal with.

The effects on oceanic fisheries are not known now, but warming could result in changing ocean currents and upwelling and thus fewer nutrients. It could alter salinity, acidity, and turbulence, bringing certain harm to the existing food chain.

These potential disruptions in human food supplies must be placed against another stark backdrop: namely the increase of the human population from just over 5 billion today to an expected 8 billion in another 40 years, an increase that will inevitably require more food.

Human health would be affected. Warming could enlarge tropical climate bringing with it yellow fever, malaria, and other diseases. Heat stress and heat mortality could rise. The harmful effects of localized urban air pollution would very likely be more serious in warmer conditions. There will be some benefits from the warming. New sea lanes will open in the Arctic, longer growing seasons further north or south will create new agricultural lands, and warmer temperatures will make some of today's colder regions more habitable. But these benefits will be in individual areas. The natural systems—both plant and animal—will be less able than man to cope and adapt. Any change of temperature, rainfall, and sea level of the magnitude now anticipated will be destructive to natural systems and living things and hence to man as well.

The list of possible consequences of global warming suggests very clearly that we must do everything we can now to understand its causes and effects and to take all measures possible to prevent and adapt to potential and inevitable disruptions triggered by global warming.

This will not be an easy matter for two reasons. First we must take such measures before we have convincing evidence that warming will have harmful impacts. Second, the human activities that are causing the temperature rise—such as burning of coal, oil, and wood and the release of other trace gases—are fundamental to the world economy. So as with the 1987 Montreal Protocol to protect the ozone layer, we will have to make a "leap of faith" to save ourselves and future generations.

As with the ozone layer, dealing with climatic changes will require the cooperation of all nations. Almost all are contributing to the problem: almost all will suffer its impacts.

(continued)

The United Nations is Acting: The first steps of the great international collaboration are being taken now within the U.N. system. To assess the scientific aspects of the problem, consider the potential effects of climate change, and identify policy options available to deal with those effects, the World Meteorological Organization (WMO), UNEP, and the International Council of Scientific Unions (ICSU) are conducting a number of studies and assessments under the umbrella of the World Climate Programme. The International Geosphere/Biosphere Programme is studying the interactions among land, the atmosphere, and the oceans. A number of national programs are being launched that will supplement this work.

The mounting concern about climate change impacts has sent storm warning flags aloft in the United Nations. . . .

The World Climate Programme is coordinated by WMO, which handles the data and applications of climate knowledge components. ICSU, WMO, and UNESCO focus on research; UNEP coordinates climatic impact studies, including the examination of food production vulnerability in climate-sensitive regions. This information will help us cope with climatic change.

We are collaborating with other international organizations, governments, and non-governmental organizations to bring together in a series of conferences and meetings the world's most distinguished experts and leading policy-makers to address the global warming issue. In 1985 the WMO-UNEP-ICSU Conference in Villach, Austria, developed—for the first time—a broad scientific consensus about anticipated global warming.

The Villach conferences established the primary direction and guidelines for UNEP's efforts. It identified issues and provided recommendations for research needed to quantify the unknowns.

Putting International Institutions in Place: Beyond gathering and disseminating scientific information, it is also imperative to organize the institutions that can direct and coordinate international efforts to deal with climate change. In addition to the World Climate Programme's scientific work, the WMO-UNEP-ICSU Advisory Group on Greenhouse Gases has been set up to advise their executive heads on global warming issues. And because ozone-depleting trace gases affect global warming, the Coordinating Committee on the Ozone Layer, set up to provide scientific assessment on the ozone layer problem, also provides assessments related to warming—including the climatic consequences of changing quantities of CFCs and tropospheric ozone.

The next major organizational step (which parallels earlier action under the ozone convention) is to bring together, within a permanent framework, the appropriate governmental experts to consider climate change. In response to decisions of their governing bodies, UNEP and WMO have formed the Intergovernmental Panel on Climate Change (IXCC), which held its first meeting in Geneva November 9–11, 1988. The IPCC will be the major intergovernmental body addressing climate change. It is comprised of governmental experts on climate change, environment, and development planning from all regions of the world. It will regularly review scientific evidence, assess social and economic impacts, and evaluate national and international policy options to address the problem.

Together, we must prepare for anticipated change, be ready to take adaptive and limitation measures . . . and capitalize on whatever benefits are possible.

At the same time, U.N. agency heads are considering possible steps that would strengthen their own cooperation on measures to address global warming.

Continuing Action Needed: These actions represent only a modest, indeed humble, start in our effort to address the world's largest and most far-reaching environmental concern. Many additional steps will be needed. The precedent established in tackling the stratospheric, ozone issue may well be a useful model for dealing with a climate.

Reprinted from William H. Mansfield III, "With a Global Focus," *EPA Journal*, October 1989, 37.

After reading these articles, you may wish to discuss this issue in small groups. Use the questions that follow to guide your discussion, or talk about other aspects of the problem.

Discussion Questions

1. Have you noticed any change in the climate in the place where you live? If so, do you feel that it may be due to the Greenhouse Effect?
2. How would some of the changes predicted in the article affect the area where you live? Would the life-style change dramatically?
3. Sometimes environmentalists seem to exaggerate when they make predictions. From what you have read, do you believe this is the case with the Greenhouse Effect?
4. Can you think of any actions you, as an individual, could take to help limit global warming?

Practice 1

The following sentences contain key words and phrases from the readings. Paraphrase the parts indicated to show that you understand their meaning. Try to do this practice without using a dictionary.

1. "Perhaps by separating the 'hard' science—*that which can be **verified** and is considered well understood*—from scientific theory or estimates, we can investigate the likelihood of near-term climate changes that have been projected."
2. "Higher CO_2 levels usually have a fertilizing effect on plants, **spurring** *them to grow faster.*"
3. "The consequences of the climate change that is currently being estimated would be enormous. **With that in mind**, it is worthwhile for us to factor climatic change into decision-making processes related to our future. . . . "
4. "International development agencies now recognize that rural people form the only labor force large enough to plant trees *on the **vast** scale that is needed.*"
5. "Protecting forests and planting trees need to be high *on the international **agenda*** for several compelling reasons. . . . "
6. "Beyond gathering and **disseminating** *scientific information*, it is also imperative to organize the institutions that can direct and coordinate international efforts to deal with climate change."
7. "These potential disruptions in human food supplies must be placed against another stark backdrop: **namely** *the increase of the human population* from just over 5 billion today to an expected 8 billion. . . . "

8. " . . . to prevent and adapt to potential and inevitable disruptions *triggered by* global warming."

9. " . . . to bring together in a series of conferences and meetings the world's most distinguished experts and leading policy-makers *to address* the global warming issue.

10. "And if we are to leave future generations a liveable world, *we have little choice but to* address climate change with all the energy, determination and wisdom we have."

Check Your Progress

Look at the following useful words from the readings. If there are any you don't recognize or know how to use, consider adding them to your vocabulary list.

READING 1

dire	modeled (v.)	productivity
feedback	posing	manipulate
model (n.)		

READING 2

catastrophic	widespread	rationale
capitalize	scenario	mobilize
magnitude	compelling	potential
decay		

READING 3

impassioned	magnitude	vulnerability
poignantly	impact	consensus
spawn	assess	precedent
stark	options	

Using a Grid to Organize Information

As you can see from your reading and discussion, although both the subject matter and even some of the vocabulary are similar, the three articles approach the subject in quite different ways. The first step in synthesizing such diverse information is to select *one* aspect of the subject which interests you. Suppose that you would particularly like to focus on the potential effects of global warming. You must skim through the articles again to discover whether this issue is discussed. To make it easy for you, those sections of each article which mention this subject are highlighted. Next, list the effects mentioned in all three articles, identifying each effect by the author who mentioned it. The following grid illustrates this process.

Possible Consequences of Greenhouse Effect	Source
1. temperature increase	Rind & Postel
2. sea level rise	Rind & Mansfield
a. threat to coastal areas	
b. warmer oceans (storms, sea life & loss of agricultural lands)	
3. more rainfall	Mansfield
4. heat-related health problems	
5. new areas open to agriculture	Mansfield
6. new habitable land	
7. plants may grow faster	Postel
8. more forests may slow warming	
9. more trees would help Third World	

Notice that some of the information that appears in one article is also reported in another, but in a somewhat different way. In the final step of synthesizing, eliminate such repetitions, and integrate the information so that your report on the Greenhouse Effect deals only with its possible effects.

Writing a Synthesis

The following summary section of the Reading Report shows how information from the three articles in this chapter might be synthesized to focus only on the effects of global warming. Because the summary section is based on information from three articles rather than just one, it consists of several paragraphs and is quite different from the original articles. Notice also that some details and examples are given.

Synthesis:
Although scientists are not certain of what the exact consequences of the Greenhouse Effect will be, it seems likely that the global warming trend will affect our lives drastically. The Greenhouse Effect is a physical process whereby the sun's energy is blocked by gases, primarily CO_2, rather than radiating back from the earth. This has caused an increase in air temperature worldwide that scientists predict will cause significant changes in the

climate throughout the world. There is uncertainty about what the eventual effects will be because no one knows how rapidly these climatic changes will take place.

There are, however, a number of theories about what will. The global air temperature may increase 1.2° C in the near future and continue to rise. If this happened, summers in Dallas, for example, would have 78 days of temperatures of 100° F or above. Warmer weather would also affect ocean currents, possibly creating more severe storms. Sea life in general would be affected, thereby causing us to lose a valuable food source. Sea levels would rise as a result of warmer weather, threatening low-lying cities such as Amsterdam and Cairo. Higher sea levels would also give off more moisture into the atmosphere, altering rainfall patterns. This, in turn, would force changes in how and where we farm as well as cause more heat-related illnesses such as malaria or heat stroke.

It seems clear that such global warming would disrupt the way we live, but some environmentalists feel that there could also be some positive results. For instance, areas formerly too cold to be inhabited or farmed could become productive. There could be longer growing seasons to provide more food. Scientists are not positive how forests and woodlands would react to a warmer climate, but there are indications that the soil might become richer and the trees that are desperately needed as an energy source in many Third World countries would grow more rapidly. Replenishing the world's depleted supply of trees would also create a natural way of placing a limit on the warming trend because increased forest land, through photosynthesis, would remove more CO_2 from the atmosphere.

Tips for Synthesizing Information

1. Choose a topic that interests you. You will be doing a lot of work with the material, and you will become bored quickly if you don't really want to learn more about the subject.
2. Make sure the readings you select all deal with your subject.
3. Read through each article without stopping to get the general idea.
4. Skim each article for information on your topic.
5. Reread each article, highlighting or marking the relevant parts.
6. Make a grid like the ones in the lesson to organize your data.
7. Use only phrases to fill in the grid; don't try to write down all the information.
8. Cross out duplicated information on the grid.
9. Check the grid for accuracy.
10. Use the grid as a plan for writing your synthesis.

Practice 2

Reread the three articles to find out how global warming might affect the area where you live, and highlight or underline the sections in each article which could be applied to your home. On the grid below, list the information along with the name of the author. When you have found as much data as you can, eliminate any facts that are mentioned in more than one article. Write a Reading Report on this aspect of the subject, synthesizing information from all three articles. Remember, your synthesis will not be like any of the articles because your emphasis is entirely different. Try to use some of the words and expressions from this lesson in your synthesis.

How Greenhouse Effect might affect (*country*)	Source

Practice 3

After practicing synthesizing skills, using the articles in this lesson, prepare another synthesis on a different topic. Because you will be locating and reading at least two articles for this assignment, select a topic that is very interesting to you. You may choose from one of the suggestions below, or you may select an entirely different topic.

Topics for Further Investigation

1. Endangered species
2. Noise pollution
3. Vegetarianism
4. Solar energy
5. Hydro-organic gardening
6. Desalinization of sea water
7. Building a space station

READING REPORT

Title _____ Author _____

Name of Publication _____ Number of Pages _____

Date of Publication _____

Type of Reading: ____ Group ____ Personal Interest ____ Academic/Serious

Source of Reading: ____ Chapter in a Book

                 ____ Newspaper Article

                 ____ Magazine Type: ____ News ____ Popular ____ Serious

                 ____ Journal Article

                 ____ Other _____

SUMMARY

RESPONSE

VOCABULARY

READING REPORT

Title _____ Author _____

Name of Publication _____ Number of Pages _____

Date of Publication _____

Type of Reading: _____ Group _____ Personal Interest _____ Academic/Serious

Source of Reading: _____ Chapter in a Book

                _____ Newspaper Article

                _____ Magazine Type: _____ News _____ Popular _____ Serious

                _____ Journal Article

                _____ Other _____

SUMMARY

RESPONSE

VOCABULARY

Name _____

Date _____

READING REPORT

Title _____ Author _____

Name of Publication _____ Number of Pages _____

Date of Publication _____

Type of Reading: _____ Group _____ Personal Interest _____ Academic/Serious

Source of Reading: _____ Chapter in a Book

_____ Newspaper Article

_____ Magazine Type: _____ News _____ Popular _____ Serious

_____ Journal Article

_____ Other _____

SUMMARY

RESPONSE

VOCABULARY

Name _____

Date _____

READING REPORT

Title _____ Author _____

Name of Publication _____ Number of Pages _____

Date of Publication _____

Type of Reading: _____ Group _____ Personal Interest _____ Academic/Serious

Source of Reading: _____ Chapter in a Book

_____ Newspaper Article

_____ Magazine Type: _____ News _____ Popular _____ Serious

_____ Journal Article

_____ Other _____

SUMMARY

RESPONSE

VOCABULARY

GROUP DISCUSSION REPORT FORM

Names of Students   Names of Articles

_____

_____

_____

_____

_____

Summary of Discussion:

Questions Raised:

GROUP DISCUSSION REPORT FORM

Names of Students   Names of Articles

_____

_____

_____

_____

_____

Summary of Discussion:

Questions Raised:

GROUP DISCUSSION REPORT FORM

Names of Students   Names of Articles

_____

_____

_____

_____

_____

Summary of Discussion:

Questions Raised:

GROUP DISCUSSION REPORT FORM

Names of Students   Names of Articles

_____

_____

_____

_____

_____

Summary of Discussion:

Questions Raised: